The Atlas of the
MEDIEVAL WORLD

J940.1
MOR

Published in the United States in 1999
by PETER BEDRICK BOOKS
A division of NTC/Contemporary Publishing Group, Inc.
4255 West Touhy Avenue, Lincolnwood (Chicago), Illinois
60646-1975 U.S.A.

The Atlas of the Medieval World in Europe was created and produced by
McRae Books Srl, via de' Rustici, 5 – Florence (Italy)
e-mail: mcrae@tin.it

Text Neil Morris, John Malam and Anne McRae
Main Illustrations Paola Ravaglia, Alessandro Cantucci, Fabiano Fabbrucci, Lorenzo
Giampaia, Andrea Morandi, Ivan Stalio, Matteo Chesi
Other illustrations Giorgio Albertini, Lorenzo Cecchi, Gian Paolo Faleschini, Michela Gaudenzi,
Jean-Marie Guillou, Sabrina Marconi, Leonardo Meschini, Federico Micheli, Donato Spedaliere
Picture research: Tatjana Marti and Marco Nardi
Graphic Design Marco Nardi
Editing Anne McRae and Cath Senker
Layout and cutouts Vincenzo Cutugno
with Adriano Nardi and Ornella Fassio
Color separations Litocolor, Florence

Printed in Italy by Grafiche Editoriali Padane, Cremona
International Standard Book Number: 0-87226-530-7

99 00 01 02 03 15 14 13 12 11 10 9 8 7 6 5 4 3 2

THE ATLAS OF THE
MEDIEVAL WORLD

in Europe (IV-XV century)

Neil Morris, John Malam, Anne McRae

Illustrations Paola Ravaglia,
Matteo Chesi, Alessandro Cantucci, Andrea Morandi

PETER BEDRICK BOOKS

NEW YORK

Contents

Vessel in the shape of a griffin used to pour water for ceremonial hand-washing. Its refinement and beauty remind us that royal courts and wealthy households maintained high and very civilized standards of living.

Throughout the Middle Ages, the majority of people lived as poor peasants. Above them on the social scale was a small class of tradesmen, monks, nuns, soldiers, and minor merchants. An even tinier group of people occupied the upper rungs of society as knights, rich bankers and merchants, important clerics, aristocrats, and princes and kings.

The medieval period was a time of innovation in the military arts and warfare. There were major improvements in weapon making, shipbuilding, protective armor, and fortification. Medieval knights wore elaborate suits of armor.

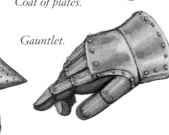

As Christianity spread, it became increasingly common for people to make journeys, often very long ones, to saints' shrines or sacred places. Pilgrims made their journeys to ask for help or forgiveness, to give thanks to God, or as simple acts of devotion.

Norman helmet wih face guard.

Great helm.

Basinet helmet with movable front piece.

Coat of plates.

Gauntlet.

Introduction

The time in European history we call the Middle Ages stretches over a period of about 1,000 years, from the fall of the Western Roman Empire in AD 476 until the great voyages of discovery and conquest in the 15th and 16th centuries. The medieval world is sometimes referred to as the "Dark Ages" and seen as a period of decline in knowledge, art, and civilization during which people lived in fear, ignorance, and poverty. As we will see in this book, this is largely untrue. The 3rd to 6th centuries were marked by widespread movements of peoples, as Germanic and Slavic clans invaded and settled within the Roman Empire. After a time of unrest most were united under Charlemagne and the Carolingians in the 9th century and a period of innovation and growth ensued. By the 11th century the population was increasing rapidly and important advances had been made in technology and learning. Although checked by the horrors of the Black Death in the 14th century, European growth and prosperity never really looked back. The 15th century was marked by the great voyages of exploration that led to European dominance of the world scene in the following centuries.

By about 600 most of Europe had been converted to Christianity. This tiny portrait on glass shows an early Christian family.

While magnifying lenses had been used for reading in China and Europe for some time, the earliest record of eyeglasses dates to 13th century Florence, in Italy.

Mosaic portrait of Tancred, the last Norman king of the Mediterranean island of Sicily. The Normans occupied Sicily for 125 years, during the 11th and 12th centuries. This is just one example of an invading people; the medieval world was marked by invasion and occupation. It was a time when entire ethnic groups moved over long distances, conquering local populations or being absorbed by them.

Advances in technology and learning were made throughout the Middle Ages. The Muslim Empire, which extended from the Near East to Spain, was an important reservoir of ancient knowledge and a hotbed of new discovery.

The first medical school was established at Salerno, in southern Italy, during the 10th century. Students came from all over Europe. It was a remarkably forward-thinking institution, even admitting woman students.

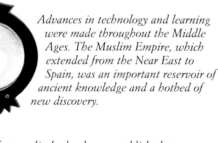

Detail from a miniature (right) showing the legendary King Arthur.

The eastern half of the Roman Empire, known as the Byzantine Empire, continued for almost a thousand years after the collapse of the western half. Its final overthrow is dated to 1453, when the Ottoman Turks took the city of Constantinople. The image (above) shows co-emperors Michael I and Leo V in 813.

Richly decorated Byzantine reliquary (container of relics) of the True Cross, now kept in Venice, Italy. Like many others of its kind, it is said to contain pieces of wood from the cross on which Jesus Christ was crucified.

This ornately carved chair was made in Piedmont, Italy, in the 15th century. The rise of a wealthy merchant class led to an increased demand for beautiful household objects and furniture.

From the 11th century onward increases in population led to rapid growth in the number and size of towns throughout Europe.

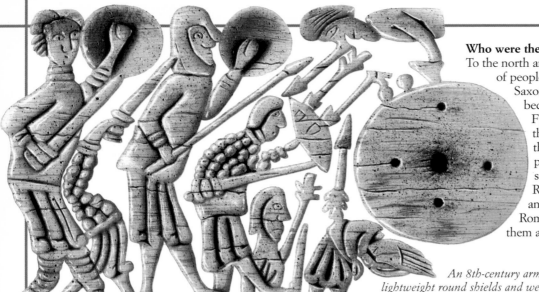

Who were the barbarians?

To the north and east of the Roman Empire were many different groups of people, such as the Goths, Vandals, Franks, Visigoths, and Saxons. The Romans referred to them all as "barbarians," because they considered their non-Latin languages uncivilized. Further away, in central Asia, lived the warlike Huns. When the Huns began to advance westward toward Europe during the 3rd to 4th centuries, they displaced all those in their path. Whole communities fled, and a tidal wave of people sought shelter inside the Roman Empire. At first the Romans tolerated the new arrivals, allowing them to settle and giving many a chance to earn their living as soldiers in the Roman army. But by the 5th century, there were too many of them and the western part of the empire was overrun.

An 8th-century army in battle. Soldiers carried lightweight round shields and were armed with long pointed swords and lances. They wore leather or iron helmets, and armor made from metal plates.

A Hun warrior's iron helmet. In the 5th century the Huns were the strongest and most feared of all the invading nations. Until Attila's defeat in 451, the Huns were the greatest danger Rome had ever faced.

The Fall of the Western Empire

From about AD 200, the once mighty Roman Empire started to weaken. It was the largest empire the world had known, but it was becoming difficult to hold together. In 284, the Emperor Diocletian divided the empire into two parts – East and West – to make it easier to control. Less than fifty years later, Rome ceased to be the capital of the Roman world. The Emperor Constantine moved the capital to the ancient city of Byzantium (modern Istanbul) in the East, which was rebuilt and renamed Constantinople. Later emperors tried to reorganize the empire; they enlarged the army, increasing taxation alarmingly to pay for it. But many were corrupt, bad leaders, and the empire continued to decline. The final blow was delivered by invaders from the north and east, whom the Romans called "barbarians." They began to enter the empire in huge numbers during the 5th century. The city of Rome itself was sacked in 410 and in 476 the western part of the empire disappeared completely when the last emperor abdicated.

By the middle of the 5th century, Gallia Belgica (modern Belgium) was occupied by the Franks, whose name meant "Free Men." Then, in 425, under their leader Chlodius, the Franks moved into Gaul (modern France). Roman cities in Gaul were weak and poorly defended, and the advance of the Franks could not be stopped. Gaul had once been a major province in the Roman Empire, but within fifty years of Chlodius' invasion, the Franks had taken it from Rome.

The Romans called Attila (c.406–53), joint king of the Huns, the "Scourge of God." He gained control of lands in the Eastern Empire, then turned on the West, but was defeated in 451 by a combined army of Romans and Visigoths. He continued to cause trouble until his death two years later.

The barbarian invaders fought from horseback using bows and arrows, shields, sabers, and lances. Among them were the Saxons, who depicted their fallen warriors on gravestones such as the one above.

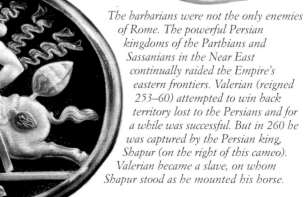

The barbarians were not the only enemies of Rome. The powerful Persian kingdoms of the Parthians and Sassanians in the Near East continually raided the Empire's eastern frontiers. Valerian (reigned 253–60) attempted to win back territory lost to the Persians and for a while was successful. But in 260 he was captured by the Persian king, Shapur (on the right of this cameo). Valerian became a slave, on whom Shapur stood as he mounted his horse.

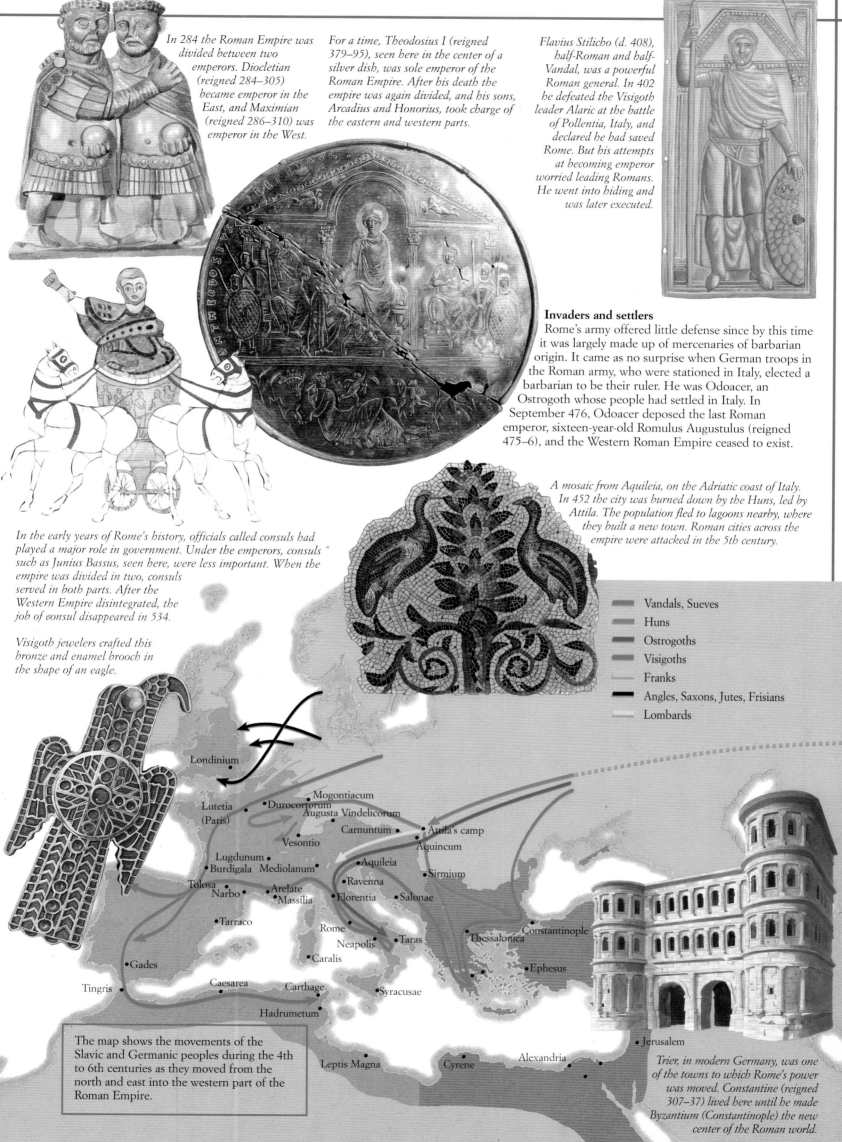

In 284 the Roman Empire was divided between two emperors. Diocletian (reigned 284–305) became emperor in the East, and Maximian (reigned 286–310) was emperor in the West.

For a time, Theodosius I (reigned 379–95), seen here in the center of a silver dish, was sole emperor of the Roman Empire. After his death the empire was again divided, and his sons, Arcadius and Honorius, took charge of the eastern and western parts.

Flavius Stilicho (d. 408), half-Roman and half-Vandal, was a powerful Roman general. In 402 he defeated the Visigoth leader Alaric at the battle of Pollentia, Italy, and declared he had saved Rome. But his attempts at becoming emperor worried leading Romans. He went into hiding and was later executed.

Invaders and settlers

Rome's army offered little defense since by this time it was largely made up of mercenaries of barbarian origin. It came as no surprise when German troops in the Roman army, who were stationed in Italy, elected a barbarian to be their ruler. He was Odoacer, an Ostrogoth whose people had settled in Italy. In September 476, Odoacer deposed the last Roman emperor, sixteen-year-old Romulus Augustulus (reigned 475–6), and the Western Roman Empire ceased to exist.

A mosaic from Aquileia, on the Adriatic coast of Italy. In 452 the city was burned down by the Huns, led by Attila. The population fled to lagoons nearby, where they built a new town. Roman cities across the empire were attacked in the 5th century.

In the early years of Rome's history, officials called consuls had played a major role in government. Under the emperors, consuls such as Junius Bassus, seen here, were less important. When the empire was divided in two, consuls served in both parts. After the Western Empire disintegrated, the job of consul disappeared in 534.

Visigoth jewelers crafted this bronze and enamel brooch in the shape of an eagle.

- Vandals, Sueves
- Huns
- Ostrogoths
- Visigoths
- Franks
- Angles, Saxons, Jutes, Frisians
- Lombards

Londinium

Lutetia (Paris)

Durocortorum

Mogontiacum

Augusta Vindelicorum

Carnuntum

Attila's camp

Aquincum

Vesontio

Lugdunum

Burdigala   Mediolanum

Aquileia

Sirmium

Ravenna

Tolosa

Narbo

Arelate

Massilia

Florentia

Salonae

Tarraco

Rome

Neapolis

Taras

Thessalonica

Constantinople

Caralis

Gades

Ephesus

Tingris

Caesarea

Carthage

Syracusae

Hadrumetum

The map shows the movements of the Slavic and Germanic peoples during the 4th to 6th centuries as they moved from the north and east into the western part of the Roman Empire.

Leptis Magna

Cyrene

Alexandria

Jerusalem

Trier, in modern Germany, was one of the towns to which Rome's power was moved. Constantine (reigned 307–37) lived here until he made Byzantium (Constantinople) the new center of the Roman world.

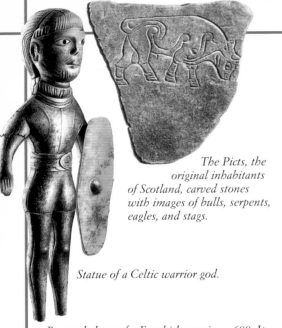

The Picts, the original inhabitants of Scotland, carved stones with images of bulls, serpents, eagles, and stags.

Statue of a Celtic warrior god.

Bronze helmet of a Frankish warrior, c.600. It must have belonged to a leading figure, since ordinary soldiers had cheaper, leather helmets.

England: Angles, Saxons, and Jutes

During the 5th to 7th centuries Britain was invaded by Angles, Saxons, and Jutes, who came from areas of northern Europe (present-day Germany and Denmark). At first they settled in the east of Britain, but as they mixed with the local population of Romanized Celts their influence spread over much of the country. Many Anglo-Saxon kingdoms emerged, which eventually united to form a single realm, called England, which meant "land of the Angles."

At Sutton Hoo, England, in about 625, an Anglo-Saxon king was buried in a ship on land. Among the objects buried with him was a pair of gold and enamel clasps for fastening an item of clothing at the shoulder.

Silver penny of Offa, King of Mercia, England (reigned 757–96).

The Germanic Kingdoms

With the Roman Empire in the West in ruins, the invading Germanic and Slavic peoples claimed its land for themselves. There followed a time of unrest, when civilization and learning took a step backward. But out of this period emerged powerful kingdoms with their own identities, languages, and cultures. It was a time when many basic features of some of the modern nations of Europe – England, France, Germany, Italy, and Spain – were forged. The fledgling states fought often among themselves and also faced outside opposition. In the 6th century, Justinian (reigned 527–65), the Emperor of the Eastern Roman Empire, tried to regain the lands lost in the West, but his success was short-lived. Only the Arabs, who occupied Spain and Portugal from the 8th to the 15th century, had more impact on the destiny of early medieval Europe.

Visigoth kings issued coins, such as Reccared I (reigned 586–601) who minted this one in Spain.

Dating from 661, the little church of San Juan de Baños de Cerrato is the finest surviving Visigoth church in Spain.

Spain: Visigoths

In the early 5th century the Visigoths settled in southern France and northern Spain. After expelling the Vandals from Spain they conquered the whole of the country. They suffered a setback in 507 when they were defeated by the Franks, who claimed all their land north of the Pyrenees. In the 6th century, civil war broke out, and rival factions contested the throne. When the last Visigoth king, Roderick (reigned 710–11), seized the throne, his opponents appealed to the Muslim leader Tarik ibn Ziyad, whose battle victory at Medina Sidonia in 711 was the start of the Arab (Moorish) conquest of Spain.

The Visigoths established their capital at Toledo, from where this example of 7th-century Christian art comes. It is a crown, which hung above a church altar.

The skill of Visigoth sculptors in Spain is clearly seen in this carved stone, or capital, which decorates the top of a column inside a church. Carved in the 7th century, it depicts a scene from the Old Testament story of Daniel in the lion's den.

France and Germany: Franks

The Kingdom of the Franks was founded by Clovis I (reigned 481–511), who adopted Christianity for his people. Between the 6th and 9th centuries the kingdom grew to include much of Christian western Europe, France, the Low Countries, Germany, Austria, Switzerland, and north and central Italy. The Franks power was at its greatest under Charlemagne ("Charles the Great," reigned 771–814), who built palaces and churches, and promoted Christianity, education, the arts, and trade. In 843 and 870 the Frankish kingdom was divided into smaller units, from which emerged the nations of France and Germany.

Throne of Dagobert I, King of the Franks (reigned 629–39), who made Paris his capital.

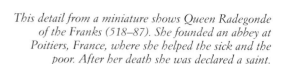

A belt buckle in silver and gold, the work of a Frankish jeweler in the 6th century.

This detail from a miniature shows Queen Radegonde of the Franks (518–87). She founded an abbey at Poitiers, France, where she helped the sick and the poor. After her death she was declared a saint.

Ornament from the helmet of Lombard King Agilulf (reigned 590–615), with figures executed in a Roman style.

Italy: Ostrogoths and Lombards

The Ostrogoths entered Italy in 489, where they established a kingdom under Theodoric the Great (reigned c.471–526). Although the Ostrogoths were of Germanic origin, they converted to Christianity early in the piece. Their kingdom collapsed in the middle of the 6th century, after which the Lombards in northern Italy gained control of the country.

The ashes of Theodoric the Great, leader of the Ostrogoths, were buried in this tomb at Ravenna, his capital in Italy.

Part of a mosaic showing Theodoric the Great's palace at Ravenna.

North Africa: Vandals

The Vandals originated in Jutland. In the early 5th century they began to migrate south through Europe. In 406 they invaded Gaul, where the Franks refused them permission to settle. They moved farther south, and in 409 reached Spain. In 429 they were driven out of Spain by the Visigoths. Under the leadership of Gaiseric, the Vandals crossed the Mediterranean to North Africa, where they defeated a Roman army. By 435 they controlled most of the Roman province of Africa, and in 439 they took the city of Carthage. The next years were spent in building a great kingdom. Their ships controlled the Mediterranean, and in 455 Vandal troops sacked Rome. In 477 Gaiseric died, and decline set in. When Carthage was captured by a Byzantine army in 533, the Vandal nation ceased to exist.

The Codex Argenteus, or "Silver Bible," was written in silver and gold letters on purple vellum in Ravenna in about 520. Of its original 336 leaves (pages), only 188 now survive.

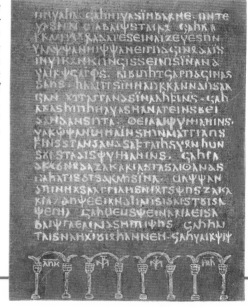

A 6th-century mosaic from Carthage, north Africa. It shows a Germanic horseman, probably a Vandal, setting out on a hunt. The craft of making mosaics was continued long after the end of Roman rule.

The Spread of Christianity

Following the journeys of Christ's apostle Paul and others in the 1st century AD, Christianity spread throughout the Roman Empire. The Christian Church began to organize provinces, with bishops at their head. The bishops of communities in the large cities of Rome, Antioch, Alexandria, and Carthage ranked highest. But at this time many Christians were persecuted, and they had to meet and worship in secret. The situation changed dramatically when the Roman Emperor Constantine became a supporter of Christianity in AD 312. Bishops and other ministers were then given special privileges, new churches and monasteries were built, and pagans were converted in large numbers. The Christian Church developed its own body of teaching, known as theology, which meant that scholars and writers could spread the word farther. The Church also had the support of Christian rulers in opposing and silencing those who believed in their own version of Christianity rather than that of the bishops. By about AD 600 most of the area of the former Roman Empire was Christian.

Saint Peter was the leader of Christ's disciples and the early Christian community in Jerusalem. According to tradition, he was crucified upside down and died a martyr in Rome during the persecution of Christians. Roman Catholics believe that Peter was chosen by Jesus as the first head of the Christian Church, and that the position of pope was established through him.

The apostle Paul spent two years as a prisoner in his own home in Rome, but he continued to preach and write to the Christian communities he had founded. Some sources say that he was released, but then arrested again before being beheaded on the orders of Emperor Nero.

Many early Christians were buried in underground cemeteries called catacombs, such as those in Rome.

By AD 312 Christianity was so widespread that it became the official Roman religion. The Roman image (right) shows a newly married couple being blessed by Christ.

Catacombs had narrow, dark passages. Burial spaces were cut into the stone walls.

The Celtic Church
Large stone Celtic crosses were carved with images of saints, as well as animals and other swirling designs. The circle around the Celtic cross came originally from a pre-Christian symbol for the Sun. In the 6th century, the influence of the Celtic Church spread from Ireland and Wales to Scotland. Columba (521–98) founded a monastery on the island of Iona, and from there missionaries traveled to northern England. The Celtic Church came into conflict with the Roman Catholic Church, and finally submitted to the authority of Rome in 768.

Early worship
As Christianity spread, its believers followed similar customs, especially those taught by the original disciples, such as Paul. One of the customs was to commemorate the Last Supper by eating bread and drinking wine (as shown in the relief, above). This was seen as a feast to show brotherhood and love among Christians, but it was not understood by many Romans, who thought such customs were dangerous secret meetings. The apostle Paul wrote to the people of Corinth, where he had founded a Christian community, telling them that they ate and drank too much at their feasts. Paul was concerned that the Corinthians were abusing their new religion.

The followers of Jesus saw him as the good shepherd. The idea of being a member of Christ's flock was very important to early Christians.

The fish was an early symbol of Christ. The Greek for fish is "ichthys," which also represented the words Iesous Christos theou hyios soter *(Jesus Christ Son of God, the Savior).*

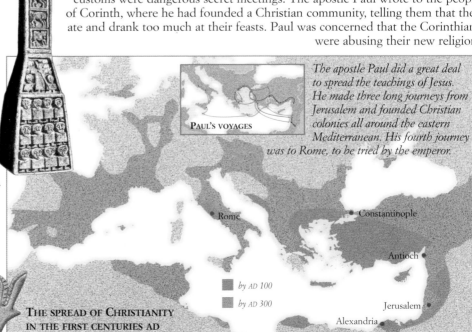

The apostle Paul did a great deal to spread the teachings of Jesus. He made three long journeys from Jerusalem and founded Christian colonies all around the eastern Mediterranean. His fourth journey was to Rome, to be tried by the emperor.

PAUL'S VOYAGES

Rome
Constantinople
Antioch
Jerusalem
Alexandria

by AD 100
by AD 300

THE SPREAD OF CHRISTIANITY
IN THE FIRST CENTURIES AD

Early Christians learned about the life of Christ from four accounts in the New Testament of the Bible. The medieval mosaic (left) shows the gospels of Matthew, Mark, Luke, and John in a wooden cupboard.

Like modern Christians, early believers thought that Jesus was the Son of God, who came to earth to lead people to salvation.

The original St Peter's Basilica was built in Rome in 333, possibly standing where the apostle Peter was buried.

This early Christian calendar followed the system devised by Julius Caesar in 46 BC. The Julian calendar lasted throughout the Middle Ages, until it was altered slightly by Pope Gregory XIII in 1582.

Mosaic of an early Christian basilica built in the Roman style.

Saint Augustine (354–430) was converted to Christianity in 386 and became Bishop of Hippo in Roman Africa. He was one of the greatest thinkers among early Christians and wrote a spiritual autobiography called Confessions.

In 313 Constantine the Great gave the Lateran Palace to the Bishop of Rome and returned seized property to Christians. The emperor also stated that Christianity was to be tolerated everywhere.

Great efforts were made to unify the early Christian Church. The illustration (right) commemorates a 4th-century council held at Nicaea, in modern Turkey, which condemned a Libyan priest named Artius for believing that Jesus was not divine.

The Syrian monk Simeon (c.390–459) became a hermit and sat on top of a tall pillar for more than 35 years (left). The snake represents worldly temptations.

In the 6th century an Italian monk named Benedict founded monasteries for those who wanted to devote themselves entirely to a religious life. This illustration shows a young Benedictine monk being taught by his superior.

Bishops, missionaries, and hermits

As Christianity spread, places of worship were built and the leading churchmen became bishops, helped by elders called presbyters and deacons. Some bishops, such as Augustine, were great scholars. Other Christians felt it more important to follow the example of Saint Paul: they became missionaries and traveled to spread the word to new places. Benedict and others founded monasteries, where Christians could lead a religious life removed from other people. Other individuals, such as Simeon, became hermits, showing their religious faith by living alone and shunning the world.

Baptisteries, like the 6th-century one shown here, were filled with water and used for baptizing people into the Christian Church. Being dipped in the water is an initiation ceremony and a symbol of being freed from sin.

Many early Christians died as martyrs. This meant they were executed for refusing to give up their faith.

This 9th-century ivory carving shows Clovis, King of the Franks, being baptized in 496. The king was converted by his wife, Clotilda, and also had 3,000 of his warriors baptized.

The Islamic World

The religion of Islam originated in Arabia in the 7th century, when the prophet Muhammad received revelations from God. Muslims, the followers of Islam, started their calendar in the year that Christians call AD 622, when Muhammad and his followers moved from Mecca, in present-day Saudi Arabia, to the oasis city of Medina. By the time Muhammad died, in 632, Islam covered most of Arabia, and it soon spread much farther afield. The Muslim Arabs were advanced in learning and technology, but they were also strong warriors who were inspired by their religious beliefs. They were generally tolerant of other people's faiths in the lands they conquered, especially those of Jews and Christians. Muslim rulers were called caliphs, and for almost six centuries they came from just two dynasties, or ruling families – the Umayyads, who moved their capital from Medina to Damascus, and the Abbasids, who ruled from Baghdad.

Muslims believe that the word of God was revealed to Muhammad in 610, when he was meditating alone in a cave on Mount Hira (above), near Mecca. A vision of the angel Gabriel called Muhammad to give God's message to his people.

Muhammad, whose face is not shown in this miniature, often dined with his followers in Mecca. Many of them were poor, for at first the prophet's teachings were not popular with rich people. They feared that they would lose their power if duty to God was thought to be more important than family or position.

A beautifully inscribed page from the Qu'ran, the sacred book of Islam. Muhammad's followers wrote down the words revealed to him by God, collected them, and arranged them into 114 chapters in around AD 650. The text is written in Arabic.

This tile reads "Allah". Arabic for "the god". Muhammad taught that Allah was the one and only God.

The cube-shaped Kaaba, in Mecca, is the most sacred Islamic shrine. It contains an ancient black stone, and Muslims all over the world face it when they pray.

Schools and learning

Before the time of Muhammad there were no schools for Arab children. But education was important to the prophet, and the Qu'ran also encourages learning. Soon Muslim scholars were respected wherever they went, and they became famous for their discoveries in astronomy, mathematics, engineering, medicine, and geography. They also copied and translated many ancient Greek manuscripts that would otherwise have been lost. Muslims built schools, universities, and libraries all over the Islamic world, and special schools called "kuttabs" were set up in mosques. About 970 the al-Azhar mosque was founded in Cairo, Egypt. Its school grew into a university, with free tuition – probably the first university in the world. Muslim universities were also founded at Baghdad, in modern Iraq, Granada in Spain, and Fez in Morocco.

The miniature (right) shows an Islamic library with Muslim scholars reading and discussing. Books are stacked on the library shelves. It comes from a manuscript produced in Baghdad in 1237.

Nomads of the Arabian Peninsula were known as Bedouin, meaning "desert dwellers." Their camels were ideally suited to the desert, and merchants traveled overland along ancient caravan routes. The Bedouin were also experienced warriors.

¡ ¿ ३ ¿ ४ ५ ६ ७ ८ ९ ०
1 2 3 4 5 6 7 8 9 0

Arabic numbers included a dot for zero. The Muslims were successful mathematicians, and they produced the first textbook on algebra in the 9th century.

The Dome of the Rock mosque in Jerusalem was built by Abd al-Malik, caliph of the ruling Umayyad dynasty, in 705. The golden-domed mosque was built over the rock on which Abraham nearly sacrificed his son, Isaac, and from where Muhammad was said to have risen to heaven.

Charlemagne, King of the Franks, fought in Spain against Muslim invaders in 778. In this French miniature his Islamic opponents are shown as frightening devils. Christians often referred to Muslims as infidels, meaning "unfaithful ones."

Followers of Muhammad build an early mosque. The first was built at Medina in 622, and was a simple rectangular building. Larger mosques are usually built around a courtyard, surrounded by arcades. The three most sacred mosques are in Mecca, Medina, and Jerusalem.

Muslim astronomers developed the astrolabe (right), to help caravan drivers find their way across the desert by studying the stars.

The Arabs developed strong ships with hinged rudders and sails that ran along the hull rather than across it. These developments made their ships, called dhows, much faster when wind conditions were not ideal.

The spiral minaret of the Great Mosque at Samarra, in present-day Iraq, was built around 850. The caliphs of the ruling Abbasid dynasty moved to this city from Baghdad at that time.

Exploration
The Arab geographer al-Idrisi was born in present-day Morocco in north Africa around 1100. He traveled throughout Europe and Asia Minor before settling at the court of King Roger II of Sicily, who asked him to produce a map of the world. Travelers were sent off on journeys of exploration, and al-Idrisi noted down everything they saw and discovered. In 1154 he produced a map (above, with north at the bottom) of the world as he knew it – north Africa, Mediterranean Europe, Arabia, Persia, and central Asia. It was remarkably accurate for its time, and even shows a possible source of the Nile River.

Narbonne

BLACK SEA

Constantinople

Cordoba
Sevilla Granada

MEDITERRANEAN SEA

Damascus Baghdad

Alexandria Jerusalem

Cairo

RED SEA

Medina

Mecca

Islam
Islam spread amazingly quickly. The whole of the Arabian peninsula was conquered by 644, and the medieval Islamic world reached its greatest extent by about 800 under the Abbasid dynasty.

Medieval Muslims were strong on everyday technology. This 12th-century candle clock had figures that popped out of a door as each hour passed.

INDIAN OCEAN

The Byzantine Empire

The Roman Empire in the East continued for almost a thousand years after the collapse of the Western Empire. Although the people of this empire still called themselves Romans, their main language was Greek rather than Latin, and we now refer to their lands as the Byzantine Empire. The Byzantines preserved Roman traditions, as well as furthering ancient Greek literature and philosophy. Christianity flourished in the Byzantine Empire, forming the basis of today's Eastern Orthodox Church. The empire constantly had to fight off threats, first from the Persians, then the Arabs, and finally from Bulgars and Turks. Invasions meant that the size of the empire varied over the centuries, but generally the Byzantine emperors ruled most of the Balkan Peninsula and Asia Minor. Turkish Muslims finally conquered Constantinople in 1453.

Religious images of Jesus and Christian saints were popular among early Byzantine artists. This icon of St Demetrius of Thessalonica is carved in soft soapstone and framed by images embossed in gilded silver.

This mosaic from a 6th-century Byzantine church in Jordan shows a plan of Jerusalem. The Holy Land was part of the empire until it was conquered by Arabs in the 7th century.

In Thessaly, Greece, Byzantine monks founded and built monasteries on top of natural sandstone pinnacles. This allowed them to escape from the everyday world and devote themselves to a religious life.

Domed stone churches were typical of Byzantine architecture. This small Byzantine church in Calabria, southern Italy, was built in the 10th century. This region, along with Sicily, first became part of the Byzantine Empire in the 6th century.

The Byzantines inherited the Ancient Romans' love of mosaics. The walls, floors, and domes of great Byzantine churches were decorated with beautiful mosaics. These were made by skilled craftsmen, who carefully set thousands of small glass and marble cubes in cement.

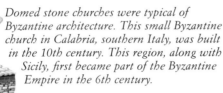

The head of Emperor Justinian I appears on this Byzantine gold coin.

Emperor Justinian I (482–565) with members of his court (left); and his wife Theodora (500–48) with a lady-in-waiting. Both are shown in beautiful Byzantine mosaics from the church of San Vitale in Ravenna, Italy.

Justinian
The Byzantine Empire was at its height under Emperor Justinian I, who ruled from 527 to 565. Justinian is most famous for his laws, his conquests, and his buildings. He appointed a group of lawyers to draw up a set of laws known as the Justinian Code. Under his leadership, Italy, part of Spain, and much of northern Africa were reconquered for the empire. He was greatly influenced by his wife, Theodora, who was very intelligent and an able politician.

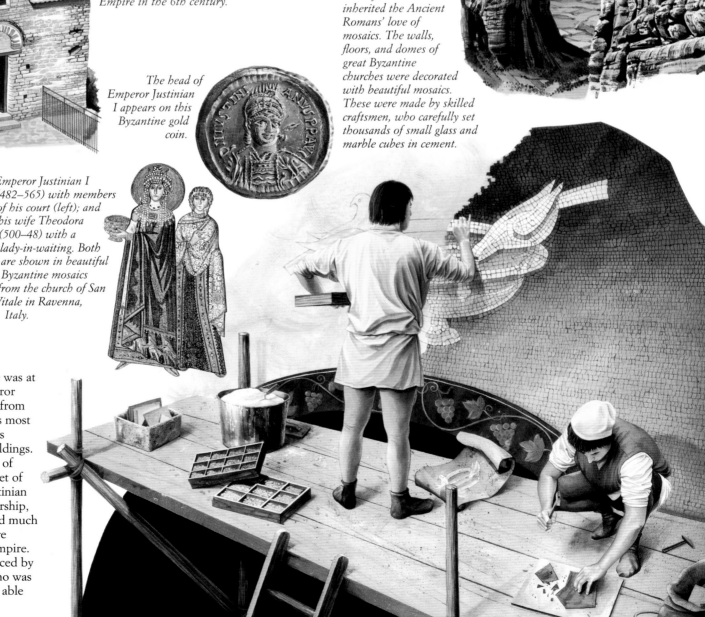

Byzantine bread was marked with a special stamp to show that it was pure and of the correct weight.

A Byzantine farmer (left) takes olive oil from an earthenware pot, while a beekeeper (right) collects honey. A form of the feudal system was introduced into the later empire.

Byzantine fishermen used lamps at night to attract fish toward their nets. This method is still used around the Aegean Sea today.

Basil the Macedonian

Basil was born a humble peasant in Thrace around 830. He succeeded in working his way up in imperial circles in Constantinople, until he became Emperor Michael III's chamberlain. Then in 866 Michael made him co-emperor. When Michael withdrew his favor a year later, Basil had him murdered. As sole emperor Basil I (below) founded the Macedonian dynasty. He made the empire more powerful in Asia Minor and southern Italy, and helped to revise the Roman law that had been set out by Justinian. Basil died on the hunting field in 886.

Fast warships

Byzantine war galleys, called "dromons," were light and fast. Many had three masts, two banks of oars each side for up to 100 rowers, and a strong ram at the bow to sink enemy ships. The Byzantines also showered enemies with a flaming mixture known as "Greek fire," which they shot from tubes on a dromon's deck. They were careful to keep the way they made the mixture a secret.

The Byzantine Empire had an organized fleet of warships and merchant vessels. A dromon was up to 160 feet long.

A carved ivory panel shows Empress Irene (c.752–803), who first ruled jointly with her son Constantine VI, but then had him imprisoned and ruled alone.

A 7th-century Byzantine coin with the head of Emperor Heraclius, who during his rule (610-41) strengthened the imperial armies.

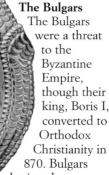

This head of Constantine the Great was once part of an enormous statue.

Hagia Sophia

Emperor Justinian I had the Church of Holy Wisdom built in Constantinople. It was completed in 537, and remained the center of the eastern Christian world for more than 900 years. The last Christian service was held there in 1453, and in the 16th century the building was converted into a mosque. Today Hagia Sophia is a museum in modern Istanbul.

The Bulgars

The Bulgars were a threat to the Byzantine Empire, though their king, Boris I, converted to Orthodox Christianity in 870. Bulgars besieged Constantinople in 813 and 913.

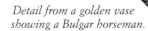

Detail from a golden vase showing a Bulgar horseman.

It took an army of 10,000 masons, carpenters, artists, and sculptors over five years to complete the beautiful Hagia Sophia in Constantinople.

This miniature of Constantinople shows the strong city walls. At the time of Justinian I the city probably had more than 500,000 inhabitants. In 542, however, an outbreak of plague killed at least half the population.

This picture of Christ (left) was disfigured by iconoclasts, who were against the worship of sacred images. The Byzantine Empire banned icons between 730 and 843 and many were damaged at this time.

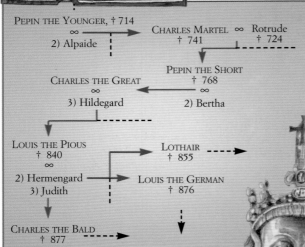

Charles Martel (c.688–741), the grandfather of Charlemagne, ruled northern Gaul and helped convert Germany to Christianity by encouraging the missionary work of Saint Boniface. Charles' son, Pepin the Short, was the first king in the Carolingian dynasty.

Charlemagne and the Frankish Kingdoms

Charlemagne was the most famous of the Carolingians, a family of Frankish kings who ruled a large part of Europe from the mid-700s to 987. When Charlemagne became ruler, in 768, he started on battle campaigns to conquer much of western Europe. He defeated the pagan Saxons in the north and the Lombards in the south. His successes meant that he doubled the territory under Carolingian control. The expanded Carolingian Empire united Europe for the first time since the end of the Roman Empire. Charlemagne was a great believer in education, and scholars at his school in Aachen collected and copied ancient Roman manuscripts. They also developed a new style of writing, called Carolingian minuscule, which later became the model for the type used in printing.

PEPIN THE YOUNGER, † 714
∞
2) Alpaide   CHARLES MARTEL ∞ Rotrude
† 741   † 724

PEPIN THE SHORT
† 768
CHARLES THE GREAT ∞
∞
3) Hildegard   2) Bertha

LOUIS THE PIOUS   LOTHAIR
† 840   † 855

2) Hermengard   LOUIS THE GERMAN
3) Judith   † 876

CHARLES THE BALD
† 877

The Carolingian dynasty was the second of the ruling Frankish families, after the Merovingians. It was founded when Pepin the Short deposed the last Merovingian king in 751. After the death of Charlemagne's son, Louis the Pious, the Carolingian Empire was split into three kingdoms.

MAVRVS·ALBINVS· SESMAR TINVS

The English educator Alcuin (c.732–804), seen here with a monk and a pupil, met Charlemagne in Italy in 781. Charlemagne made him head of the school he set up at Aachen.

Paderborn
Aachen
Prague
Mainz
Paris   Verdun
Metz
Strasbourg
Augsburg
Poitiers
Milan
Pavia
Roncesvalles
Narbonne
Rome

Charles the Great

About 742, probably in Aachen, Pepin the Short's wife, Bertha, gave birth to her first son. The boy was named Karl, or Charles, and he was to become one of the greatest kings of the Middle Ages. In 768, Charles inherited half of his father's Frankish kingdom. When his younger brother died three years later, Charles took the other half too and became King of the Franks. Charlemagne, or Charles the Great, became Roman Emperor in 800. Charles died in 814, and his son Ludwig, or Louis the Pious, became emperor but proved to be a weak ruler.

This horseman and his mount formed a decorative emblem on a Lombard shield. The rider has his lance lowered for action.

Charlemagne standardized the currency of much of Europe, which was based on a silver coin called a denier. This one (above) was minted around 804 in Frankfurt. After the Middle Ages the European currencies split up again, until they were reunited by the Euro (above, right) at the end of the 20th century.

The Lombards

Charlemagne fought and defeated the Lombards of northern Italy in a long campaign during 773–4. The Lombards had become enemies of the pope, who asked for the Carolingians' help. When Charlemagne became King of the Lombards, his friendship and alliance with the pope were strengthened.

The gatehouse of the monastery of Lorsch, a village near Worms, in Germany. The monastery was founded in the 8th century, and the entrance is based on ancient triumphal arches. Carolingian architects tried to copy early Christian buildings, but at the same time their works had a German look.

Roman Emperor

In 800, Charlemagne journeyed to Rome. On Christmas Day, Pope Leo III put a jeweled crown on his head and declared him emperor of the Romans. Historians sometimes call Charlemagne's empire the Western Roman Empire, to show that it was separate from the Byzantine Empire in eastern Europe, which had its own ruler in Constantinople. Later, Charlemagne's western empire was called the Holy Roman Empire, showing how closely tied it was to the power and influence of the pope and the Christian religion. After his coronation in 800, Charlemagne stayed in Rome for four months and condemned all the pope's enemies as rebels.

This 9th-century bronze statue of Charlemagne is in the Louvre museum, in Paris.

Between 790 and 805 Charlemagne had a complex of buildings constructed in the capital of his kingdom, Aachen. He wanted the buildings to serve as his royal court and national church. Among them was the Palatine Chapel, which still stands as the most important example of Carolingian architecture. The chapel was modeled on a church in Ravenna, Italy, and at almost 100 feet it was for many centuries the tallest stone building in Germany.

The imperial crown, sceptre, sword, ring, and orb showed the power of the Holy Roman Empire. This jeweled iron crown was worn by the emperor from the 11th century, and the gold orb was added a hundred years later. The cross shows the link with the Christian Church.

This Frankish sword and scabbard were found buried in a royal tomb in France. The sword was an important symbol of royalty and power.

Charlemagne could read and speak Latin, but he never learned to write it. He signed his name by making a cross with the letters "KRLS," which became his monogram.

The noblewoman Dhuoda was married to Bernard, Count of Barcelona, the son of Charlemagne's cousin. Dhuoda's two sons were both taken away from her by her husband. Around 830 she wrote a book giving her older son advice on how to live a good life by respecting authority, worshiping God, and reading.

An illuminated page (below) from one of the Golden Gospels that were written and illustrated at Charlemagne's school in Aachen. They were written mainly in gold on purple-stained vellum. This illustration shows Saint Luke.

This document, called the Strasbourg Oaths and dating from 842, is the text of oaths sworn by two of Charlemagne's grandsons, Charles the Bald and Louis the German. It is thought to be the first written document in the French language.

In the summer of 778, Charlemagne's army was returning from a failed campaign in Spain. In the Pyrenees mountains, the Frankish army was attacked by Basques. An officer called Count Hruodland (left) was killed.

The Carolingian empire

By 800 Charlemagne ruled over most of western Europe. His kingdom covered most of the area covered by modern France, Belgium, the Netherlands, Switzerland, Austria, Germany, the Czech Republic, Slovenia, northern Italy, and part of Spain. Charlemagne divided the kingdom into districts, and each was governed on his behalf by a count. Ambassadors traveled throughout the empire to make sure that the king's orders were obeyed. Bishops were put in charge of Church matters. A rough set of laws was used throughout the empire, and though many of the laws were harsh, most thought they were also fair. Charlemagne encouraged farming, trade, learning, and religion among his people.

The Franks made use of special pieces of military equipment – wooden armored carriages. These must have been very effective in the many wars they fought. Charlemagne waged his longest campaign against the Saxons of northern Germany. After many years of war, he at last defeated them and forced them to accept Christianity in 804. Over 32 years, Charlemagne took the field against the Saxons 18 times.

Song of Roland

More than 300 years after the battle against the Basques in the Pyrenees (see text above), Count Hruodland became famous as Roland, the hero of France's greatest epic poem. *The Song of Roland* was written by an unknown French author. In the poem, the courageous Roland is betrayed by a traitor. The officer shows great devotion to Charlemagne, but dies in a battle against the Muslims.

Life in the Country

In the Middle Ages, most people in Europe lived in villages and worked on the land. Each village was controlled by a lord of the manor, who lived in a big house and owned all the land. Peasant farmers were known as serfs or villeins. They had to do everything they were told by their local lord, who allowed them to work strips of land in his fields, in order to feed themselves. But they had to pay a tax by giving him some of the food they grew, as well as paying a "tithe," a tenth of their produce, to the Church. This meant that life was a hard struggle, and peasants worked all daylight hours throughout the whole year, just to grow enough to feed their families. They lived in villages in small, simple houses made of mud and turf, with a wooden frame and a thatched roof. In bad years when crops failed, families simply starved and many fell ill and died.

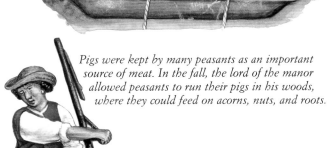

Pigs were kept by many peasants as an important source of meat. In the fall, the lord of the manor allowed peasants to run their pigs in his woods, where they could feed on acorns, nuts, and roots.

Ordinary farmers did not own a plow (below), which was used for cutting furrows in the soil and turning it over before sowing seed. Plows usually belonged to the local lord, or were owned by all the people of a village. During harvesting, workers were watched over by the lord's reeve, or supervisor.

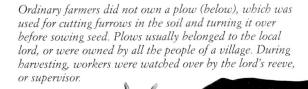

All cutting and harvesting work was done by hand, using simple tools like these. There were no machines to help, so it was back breaking work for the peasants.

Three-field system

The crop-growing areas around medieval villages were usually divided into three big fields. The lord of the manor allowed peasants to work strips in each of the fields, so that good and bad soil was shared fairly between them. The farmers used the three fields very cleverly, to get the most out of them. Every year, one field was sown with wheat, the second with barley, and sometimes rye and oats, and the third field was plowed but left fallow, or unplanted. The following year, the fallow field was more fertile, and this system meant that each field had a chance to recover its fertility every three years. Changing the crops around also helped to make them grow better.

Harvest time

For most of the year farmers spent their time working their own small strips of land in three big fields. But at harvest time, in the fall, all the villagers worked together, because there was so much to do in a short time. This happened in other seasons too, if farmers were able to raise more than one crop a year. Women and children helped by cutting the wheat and other cereals with sickles, and tying it in bundles. Then they loaded the bundles onto carts and took them to the barn. The cereal then had to be threshed, to separate the grain from the stalks. This was done by beating it with a stick. The leftover stalks, or straw, were useful too. Straw could be used to thatch roofs and make mattresses.

Wool was an extremely valuable trading product in the Middle Ages, so sheep shearing was an important job. Peasant women used hand-held spindles to spin the wool into a coarse thread. Some unmarried women made a living in this way, and they became known as "spinsters."

When it came to harvest time, women and children helped the men in the fields.

Thread was woven into cloth and then made into clothes. Weaving was done on hand looms, like the 15th-century one these women are using (right). By that time, many weavers had set up businesses in towns.

Bees were kept for their honey, which was used to sweeten food.

Milk from cows, sheep, and goats was used to make cheese, which was known as "white meat." Peasants made their own cheese, and in the fast-growing towns, people opened specialist cheese and dairy shops.

Cooking cauldron
Villagers boiled most of their food. They put different foods in an iron cauldron (right), which was filled with water and hung over an open fire. Meat such as ham or bacon was put at the bottom. Eggs, poultry, and fish were boiled in earthenware pots, and puddings in sacks. The cauldron was hung from a hook on a ratchet, so that it could be raised or lowered over the fire.

Poor countryfolk beg for food in this painting by the Italian medieval artist Andrea Orcagna (c.1308–68). Life was always hard in the country, and if a harvest failed, it had disastrous effects on people.

This Romanesque sculpture shows men picking and weighing grapes to make into wine. Wine had been made in many parts of Europe since Greek and Roman times, or even earlier.

These illustrations from around 1300 show some of the goods that peasants had to pay to the lord of the manor.

Many peasants had a small vegetable plot and garden next to their house. They grew herbs as well as cabbages and peas.

A peasant family in front of their simple house. Village people had to make almost everything for themselves. The man is using twigs to make a wicker basket. His wife is making butter, which was a long, tiring job. Children were given plenty of jobs to do, including looking after the family's animals.

The Invasions of the 9th and 10th Centuries

Under Carolingian rule, Christian churchmen and noblemen became more wealthy throughout Europe. This wealth encouraged invaders to attack from three different directions. From the north came the Vikings. Toward the end of the 8th century they sailed in their fast longships from Denmark, Norway, and Sweden, raiding coasts and making settlements in such places as Dublin in Ireland, York in England, and Normandy in France. At the same time, Arab Saracens attacked from the south and had a great influence on southern Europe for about 200 years. From the end of the 9th century, the third set of invaders, the Magyars, rode in from the east. They led successful raids on central Europe for over 50 years, before being defeated by the Holy Roman Empire.

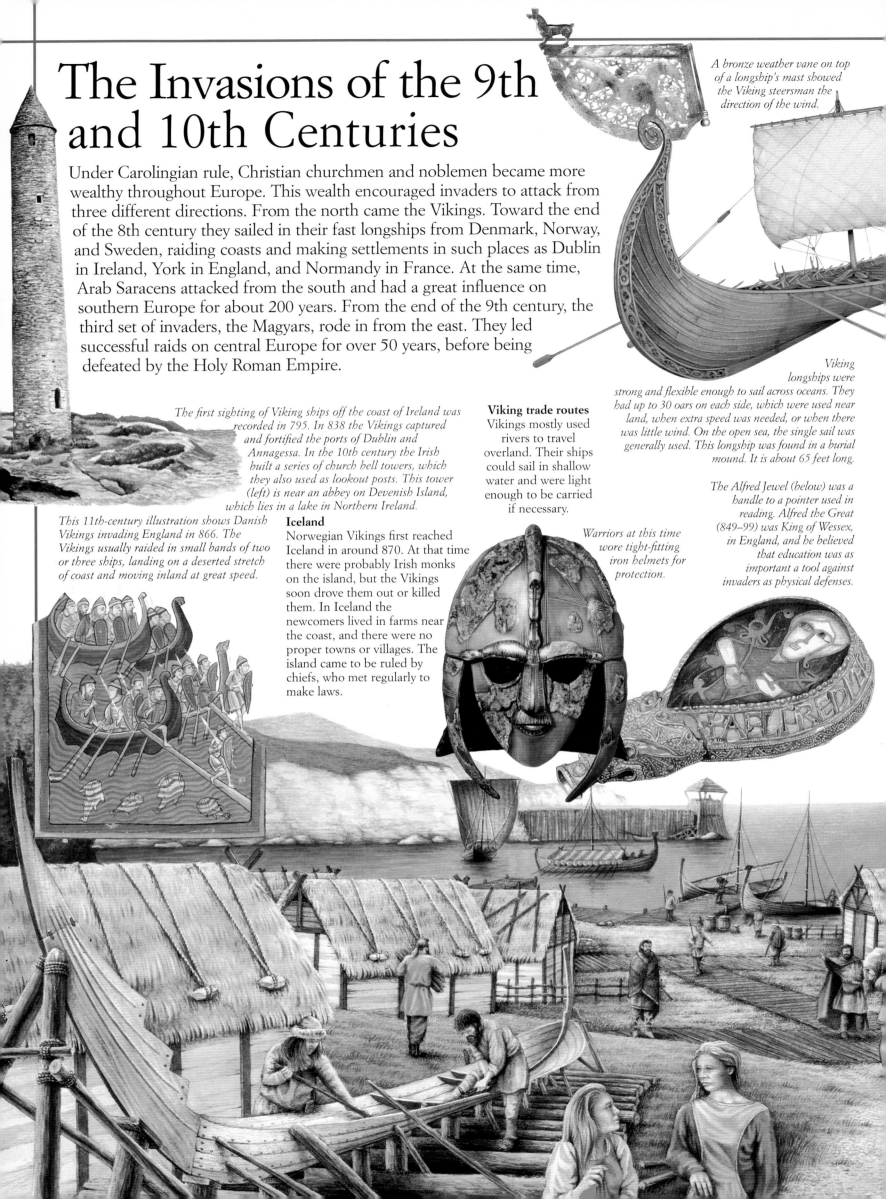

A bronze weather vane on top of a longship's mast showed the Viking steersman the direction of the wind.

The first sighting of Viking ships off the coast of Ireland was recorded in 795. In 838 the Vikings captured and fortified the ports of Dublin and Annagessa. In the 10th century the Irish built a series of church bell towers, which they also used as lookout posts. This tower (left) is near an abbey on Devenish Island, which lies in a lake in Northern Ireland.

Viking longships were strong and flexible enough to sail across oceans. They had up to 30 oars on each side, which were used near land, when extra speed was needed, or when there was little wind. On the open sea, the single sail was generally used. This longship was found in a burial mound. It is about 65 feet long.

Viking trade routes
Vikings mostly used rivers to travel overland. Their ships could sail in shallow water and were light enough to be carried if necessary.

This 11th-century illustration shows Danish Vikings invading England in 866. The Vikings usually raided in small bands of two or three ships, landing on a deserted stretch of coast and moving inland at great speed.

Iceland
Norwegian Vikings first reached Iceland in around 870. At that time there were probably Irish monks on the island, but the Vikings soon drove them out or killed them. In Iceland the newcomers lived in farms near the coast, and there were no proper towns or villages. The island came to be ruled by chiefs, who met regularly to make laws.

Warriors at this time wore tight-fitting iron helmets for protection.

The Alfred Jewel (below) was a handle to a pointer used in reading. Alfred the Great (849–99) was King of Wessex, in England, and he believed that education was as important a tool against invaders as physical defenses.

Vikings
Saracens
Magyars

The Saracens

The Saracens were Muslim Arabs, originally from the Arabian peninsula, who from the 7th century spread the Islamic religion across northern Africa and then to Spain. In the 9th century they captured Sicily, and they went on to make bases in southern Italy, Sardinia, Corsica, and southern Gaul.

Stephen I (c.975–1038) was the son of the Magyar prince Geza. After being brought up as a Christian, Stephen defeated a pagan revolt in 998. Two years later he became the first king of Hungary. He was made a saint in 1083, and is still a national hero in Hungary today.

The Magyars

These were nomadic horseriding tribes from the East, who moved into the plains of Hungary in the 9th century. From there they invaded northern Italy, Germany, and central France. Their great horsemanship made them fast moving and very difficult to stop, but they were finally defeated by the Holy Roman Emperor in 955. The Magyar leaders were killed, and the rest were forced to become Christians and join with Western Rome against Eastern Byzantium. By the year 1000, the first king of Hungary had made the home of the Magyars a Christian country.

In Sicily, the heroic deeds of medieval knights were acted out in puppet theaters. One of the favorite characters was Roland (left), whose brave exploits were described in heroic poetry.

Saracens (below) from north Africa first attacked Sicily in 827, when it was under the rule of the Byzantine Empire. The Saracens ruled for about 200 years.

Arab influence

Many areas of southern Europe, such as Sicily, were greatly influenced by Muslim art, literature, and science. This casket (above) is decorated in an Arab style, and this medieval church in Palermo (lower left) also shows a strong Arab influence. The Saracens brought their methods of irrigation to the island, and began growing crops such as oranges, lemons, and cotton.

Stephen I was crowned on Christmas Day, 1000, with the approval of Pope Sylvester II. It is said that the pope even sent the crown, which later became a Hungarian national treasure. The crown (right) is made from an 11th-century jeweled circlet, to which round and triangular plates of enameled gold were added in the 12th century.

Coastal settlements

The Vikings made settlements near the coast, both at home in Scandinavia and when they traveled. Their wooden houses had roofs covered in turf. Early towns had markets, where people traded furs, textiles, and iron. One of the earliest Scandinavian towns, Hedeby in Denmark, began as a small Viking settlement in the 8th century.

The Magyars were finally defeated at the Battle of Lechfeld, in Germany, by the army of Otto I (912–73), who was then Holy Roman Emperor. It is believed that Otto carried this holy lance (left), which was supposed to contain a piece of wood from the cross on which Christ was crucified.

Europe in the Year 1000

In AD 1000 the people of Europe numbered less than 40 million. Today, there are more than twelve times as many people across the continent. But at the end of the first millennium the population started to grow quite rapidly. In most countries, settled governments and freedom from expensive wars led to stability and growth. More food was needed to feed the growing population, and new lands were cleared for farming. At the same time farming methods improved throughout Europe, which meant that markets in towns and villages became more important. People were able to travel between towns, and they no longer felt so tied to their own home. Traders were happy to travel long distances to buy and sell their goods. Many other travelers were Christian pilgrims, who made their journeys to holy places. They traveled to show their devotion to God, to be forgiven for their sins, or sometimes in an attempt to be cured of an illness. It was a time of important political changes, too. William of Normandy invaded England in 1066, and brought the feudal system to his newly conquered lands.

Farmers had to carry their grain to their lord's mill for it to be ground into flour. Water was an important source of power in the Middle Ages. Watermills were set up along streams and rivers with strong currents.

This image from the Baptistery of St John in Florence, Italy, shows how medieval people feared they might be caught, and even eaten, by the Devil. The Baptistery was built around the year 1000 as a place to baptize people.

All sorts of goods were sold on market day in the towns, when traders set up their stalls. As trade increased, the markets became more important and the towns grew bigger.

Pilgrims on their way

Most pilgrims made their way along roads and paths on foot, but wealthier pilgrims rode on horseback. They usually traveled in groups, for safety. The three main routes of pilgrimage led to Santiago de Compostela in Spain (see map below), to Rome, where both Saint Peter and Saint Paul were believed to be buried, and across the Mediterranean Sea to the Holy Land. It was the greatest wish of all Christians to visit Jerusalem, but few managed such a long journey. In England many pilgrims journeyed to the market and cathedral city of Canterbury. On their way, pilgrims told stories and sang songs and hymns. Geoffrey Chaucer's famous book, *The Canterbury Tales*, is full of stories told by pilgrims on their way to that city.

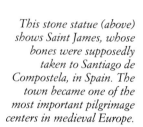

This relic, from Assisi in Italy, is said to contain a thorn from the crown that Christ wore when he was crucified. Assisi was the birthplace of Saint Francis of Assisi (c.1181–1226), and has been a place of pilgrimage since the Middle Ages.

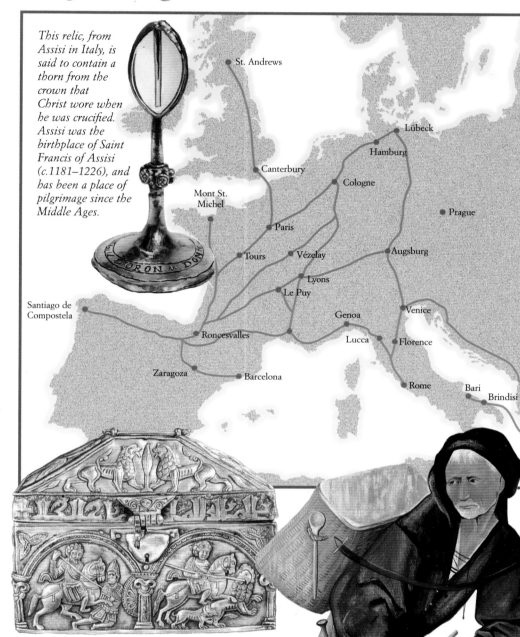

St. Andrews
Lübeck
Hamburg
Canterbury
Cologne
Mont St. Michel
Prague
Paris
Tours
Vézelay
Augsburg
Lyons
Le Puy
Santiago de Compostela
Genoa
Venice
Roncesvalles
Lucca
Florence
Zaragoza
Barcelona
Rome
Bari
Brindisi

The map shows the main pilgrim routes through France and northern Spain to Santiago de Compostela.
The town of Vézelay, in France, grew up around a Benedictine abbey, which was supposed to contain the remains of St Mary Magdalene.

This stone statue (above) shows Saint James, whose bones were supposedly taken to Santiago de Compostela, in Spain. The town became one of the most important pilgrimage centers in medieval Europe.

Pilgrims were frequently attacked by robbers. Wealthy pilgrims took an armed escort with them, to avoid such incidents.

Saint Stanislaus

This casket, called a reliquary, is said to contain the remains of Saint Stanislaus, the patron Saint of Poland. Stanislaus (1030–79), bishop of Krakow, was murdered after he opposed the reputedly cruel King Boleslaw II of Poland, known as the Bold. Stanislaus was declared the first Polish saint in 1253.

The Prodigal Son, painted by the Dutch artist Hieronymus Bosch (c.1450–c.1516) and based on the Bible story. The wasteful son is returning home after spending years away from his father's house. Many travelers covered long distances during the Middle Ages, staying in taverns on their way. Pedlars sold goods in the towns and villages as they passed through.

The Bayeux tapestry

The Bayeux tapestry is an embroidered linen strip. It is 230 feet long and 20 inches in depth. The 72 scenes of the 11th-century tapestry show how England was conquered by William I (1028–87), Duke of Normandy, who earned the name William the Conqueror. It starts with King Harold's visit to Normandy and ends with the Battle of Hastings. It used to be thought that the tapestry was woven by Matilda, wife of William the Conqueror, but it is now believed that it was made later. The tapestry may have been commissioned by William's half brother, the bishop of Bayeux, in France, where it can still be seen.

The Bayeux tapestry (right) shows many scenes of the Norman conquest of England, in 1066.

A RECONSTRUCTION OF THE MONASTERY OF CLUNY

The largest and most important building in a monastery was the church. Monks prayed there at various times during the day and night.

Saint Bernard of Clairvaux (1090–1153), the son of a French nobleman, founded a Cistercian monastery and helped to expand that religious order.

Medieval monks could walk, sit or read in the cloister, a covered walkway next to an open square.

During the Middle Ages Christians honored the Virgin Mary, the mother of Jesus, more and more. Many thought that she could help them to win God's favor. The Madonna and Child (Mary and Jesus) was a favorite subject for medieval artists.

Burning incense was placed inside this censer. During mass, a priest swung the censer from its golden chain, to spread smoke from the incense and fill the church with a sweet smell. Monks worshiped God constantly, and other churchgoers believed that they would be rewarded by God if they attended mass regularly.

In 1209 Giovanni di Bernadone (c.1181–1226), who is known as St Francis of Assisi (left), founded the Franciscan order of friars. Six years later he helped St Clare of Assisi (right) set up a convent for nuns. Both gave away all their possessions and traveled around, spreading their beliefs. Because she once saw mass celebrated at a distance, St Clare was made patron saint of television in 1958.

The Religious Life

In the 6th century an Italian monk named Saint Benedict drew up a set of regulations for those who wanted to devote themselves to religion and lead a Christian life. The "Rule" of Saint Benedict told monks and nuns to make three vows – to give up everything they owned, to obey their superiors, and never to marry. Those who followed the "Rule" joined the order of the Benedictines. They lived apart from other people, in their own community: monks in monasteries, and nuns in convents. Their days were divided into special times for prayer, study, and work. Over the centuries some Benedictine monasteries became rich, as land was left to them when people died. The monks were able to hire workers to help them. In 1098, French monks called Cistercians moved to more remote places and did all the work themselves. Another order, the Carthusians, thought that the best way to serve God was by a life of silent prayer. The numbers of monks, nuns, and religious orders continued to grow throughout the Middle Ages.

Caterina Benincasa (1347–80) was born in Siena, Italy. She was said to have seen a vision of Christ when she was six, and at the age of sixteen she joined the Dominican order of nuns. Caterina spent most of her life caring for sick and poor people, such as this beggar (above). It was said that the marks of Christ's crucifixion appeared on her body in 1375. She was made a saint in 1461 and named Saint Catherine of Siena.

Illuminated manuscripts

These manuscripts were books written and illustrated by hand. They were illuminated, which means "lit up" or decorated, with pictures in bright colors and gold and silver. They were also called miniatures. The most common illuminated manuscripts were Bibles, prayer books called Books of Hours, collections of psalms called psalters, chronicles, and poetry. Initial letters were decorated with beautiful designs, and some large letters had illustrations within them. The illuminations were usually added after the text had been written by a scribe. The pages were made of parchment, the dried skin of a sheep or goat. The decorations were done in thick watercolor paint, and illuminators especially prized a brilliant shade of blue made from a gem called lapis lazuli. The red color, called minium, came from lead. Illuminators also used gold leaf, which was made by beating a tiny piece of gold until it became thinner than paper. The gold leaf was stuck on the page and then rubbed down to make it shiny.

Decorated initial

Parchment page

Border decoration

This Italian illuminated manuscript tells the legend of Saint George in words and pictures. According to the legend, Saint George saved a king's daughter by killing a fierce dragon with his lance.

Music was very popular in medieval churches. Monks recited texts by chanting them in a single key. This is called plainsong, and its most famous form is Gregorian chant, named after Pope Gregory I. In this picture from an earthenware plate, a monk plays the organ, while a servant pumps the bellows to make the instrument work. A choirboy sings, and the dog seems to be joining in too.

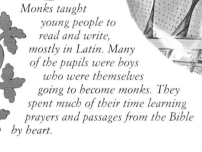

Monks taught young people to read and write, mostly in Latin. Many of the pupils were boys who were themselves going to become monks. They spent much of their time learning prayers and passages from the Bible by heart.

Monks farmed the land, and many monasteries produced all their own food. There was a great deal of work to do at planting and harvest time. There was often a barn in the monastery, where hay was stored. Monks made their own bread and even beer.

This monk is copying out a manuscript, while others work in the monastery's vegetable garden. Monasteries had a special room set aside for writing, called a scriptorium, while finished books were kept in the library. Monks who acted as scribes spent hours each day copying out religious texts in beautiful script. The texts were usually in Latin. The scribes used pointed quills, made from goose feathers, which they sharpened with a penknife. If they made a mistake, they scraped it off the parchment with the knife. The monk's sloping desk made his work easier.

These monks are collecting wood from the forest for carpentry. They were sometimes helped by lay brothers, who had taken holy vows but were not well-educated enough to be monks.

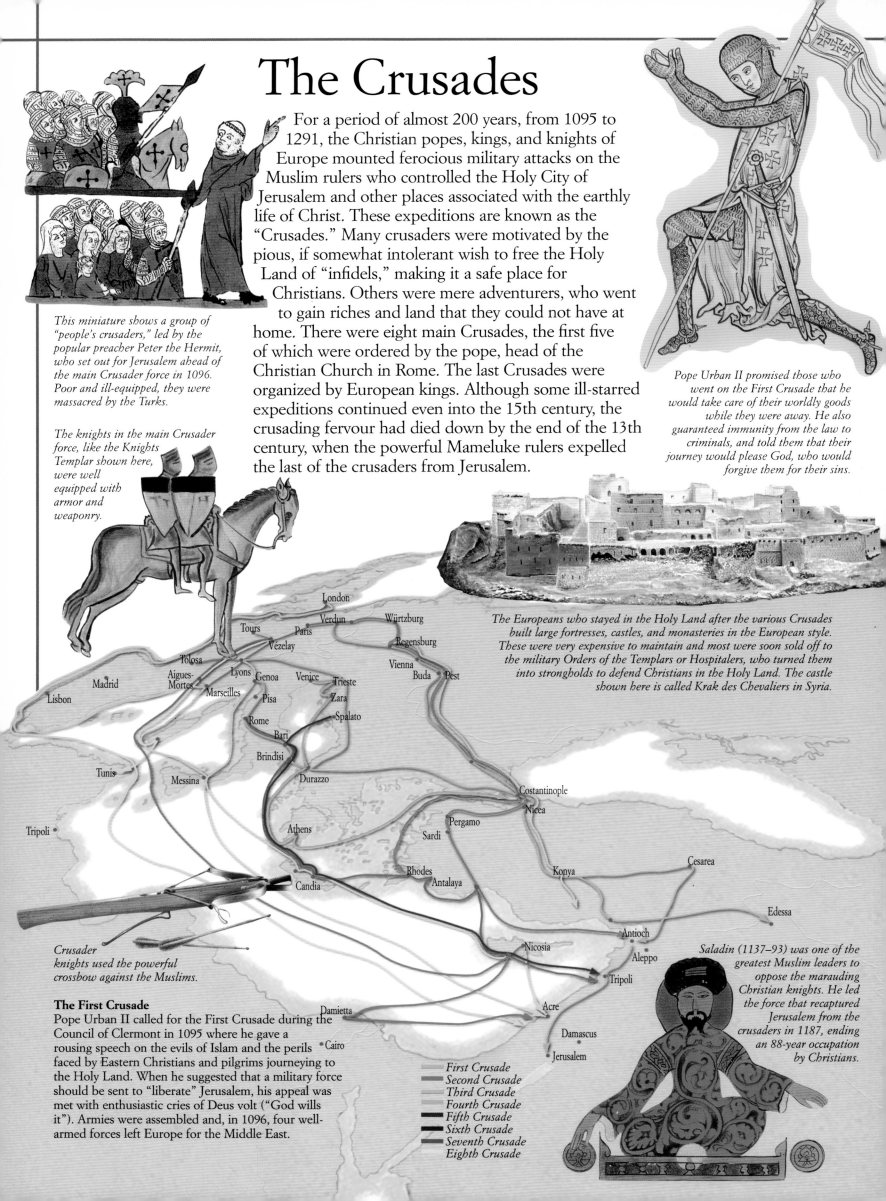

The Crusades

For a period of almost 200 years, from 1095 to 1291, the Christian popes, kings, and knights of Europe mounted ferocious military attacks on the Muslim rulers who controlled the Holy City of Jerusalem and other places associated with the earthly life of Christ. These expeditions are known as the "Crusades." Many crusaders were motivated by the pious, if somewhat intolerant wish to free the Holy Land of "infidels," making it a safe place for Christians. Others were mere adventurers, who went to gain riches and land that they could not have at home. There were eight main Crusades, the first five of which were ordered by the pope, head of the Christian Church in Rome. The last Crusades were organized by European kings. Although some ill-starred expeditions continued even into the 15th century, the crusading fervour had died down by the end of the 13th century, when the powerful Mameluke rulers expelled the last of the crusaders from Jerusalem.

This miniature shows a group of "people's crusaders," led by the popular preacher Peter the Hermit, who set out for Jerusalem ahead of the main Crusader force in 1096. Poor and ill-equipped, they were massacred by the Turks.

The knights in the main Crusader force, like the Knights Templar shown here, were well equipped with armor and weaponry.

Pope Urban II promised those who went on the First Crusade that he would take care of their worldly goods while they were away. He also guaranteed immunity from the law to criminals, and told them that their journey would please God, who would forgive them for their sins.

The Europeans who stayed in the Holy Land after the various Crusades built large fortresses, castles, and monasteries in the European style. These were very expensive to maintain and most were soon sold off to the military Orders of the Templars or Hospitalers, who turned them into strongholds to defend Christians in the Holy Land. The castle shown here is called Krak des Chevaliers in Syria.

Crusader knights used the powerful crossbow against the Muslims.

Saladin (1137–93) was one of the greatest Muslim leaders to oppose the marauding Christian knights. He led the force that recaptured Jerusalem from the crusaders in 1187, ending an 88-year occupation by Christians.

The First Crusade

Pope Urban II called for the First Crusade during the Council of Clermont in 1095 where he gave a rousing speech on the evils of Islam and the perils faced by Eastern Christians and pilgrims journeying to the Holy Land. When he suggested that a military force should be sent to "liberate" Jerusalem, his appeal was met with enthusiastic cries of Deus volt ("God wills it"). Armies were assembled and, in 1096, four well-armed forces left Europe for the Middle East.

First Crusade
Second Crusade
Third Crusade
Fourth Crusade
Fifth Crusade
Sixth Crusade
Seventh Crusade
Eighth Crusade

The Crusader kingdoms

The First Crusade conquered Jerusalem on July 15, 1099. The crusaders slaughtered the Muslim and Jewish inhabitants of the city. Over the following years, they gained control of a narrow coastal strip of Palestine and set up the so-called "Crusader kingdoms," under the control of European leaders.

The crusaders of the Fourth Crusade plundered the city of Constantinople. These horses were brought back to the Italian city of Venice, where they are still to be seen today.

This miniature shows a lance-bearing Christian force struggling against Muslim warriors during the Second Crusade, in 1147–8.

Below: crosses scratched into the walls of the Church of the Holy Sepulcher in Jerusalem by crusaders are still visible today.

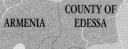

The map below shows Jerusalem at the center of the world. At that time Christian maps were all drawn like this because Jerusalem was the site of the Church of the Holy Sepulchre, where Jesus was buried.

The crusading fervor led to a Children's Crusade in 1212, when thousands of European children set off for the Holy Land. The children were all lost or sold into slavery.

Many Jews fell to the crusaders' swords, as well as Muslims.

Saladin's armies had more sophisticated means of communication than their European opponents. They used beacon fires and smoke signals as well as a pony express system and even pigeon post (although the crusaders' trained falcons often intercepted messages sent by pigeon).

Cultural exchange

Although Christians and Muslims were bitter enemies, nonetheless they learned from one another during the Crusades. Europeans adopted the use of insignia (symbols) to identify different groups of knights, and these became the basis of Western heraldry.

The Fourth Crusade

Pope Innocent III called the Fourth Crusade against Egypt in 1198. The resulting crusader army was very poor so, in exchange for ships and weapons, the crusaders agreed to help the powerful trading town of Venice to conquer the city of Constantinople. This led to the definitive split between the Latin Church, based in Rome, and the Byzantine one, based in Constantinople.

After months or years on a crusade, the knights returned home to their feudal homes and families. This statue shows Hugo de Vaudemont with his wife on his return after the conquest of Jerusalem during the First Crusade.

During the crusader period, Europeans learned from the Muslims how to use carrier pigeons as messangers.

Crusader knights also brought a taste for new foods and spices back with them from the East. Candied fruit and sugar were introduced into Europe at this time.

The crusaders brought knowledge back from the East, including the technology required to run a windmill.

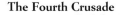

The Black Death: Medicine and Science

When a terrible plague called the Black Death struck Europe in the 14th century, people were completely unable to understand or fight it. Knowledge of science and medicine was slowly spreading among the universities that were opening all over the continent, but even trained doctors had no understanding of how such a disease spread. Many believed that this was a disaster sent by God to punish people for their wickedness. Groups of people called flagellants wandered from town to town, whipping themselves to try and make amends for human sins. Meanwhile, European scholars were continuing to learn from each other and from people in other parts of the world, and some tried to unite their growing knowledge with the teachings of the Church.

This strange-looking character is a medieval doctor. He is wearing protective clothing against disease. Most people believed that the Black Death was caused by bad air, but they came to realize that the disease could be passed on by contact with a victim.

The victims of the plague (right) suffered an extremely painful but quick death. Because of the number of deaths, many people were buried in mass graves.

SPREAD OF BLACK DEATH
(by date)

■	1346
	1347
	1348
	1349
	1350
	1351
	Areas with little or no plague

Spreading death

The Black Death, or bubonic plague, came from central Asia and spread to Europe in 1347. Three years later it had killed millions of people in Europe. At least a third of the population died. The disease was passed on to humans by deadly bacteria: first a flea bit an infected rat, and then the flea passed the bacteria on when it bit a person. People in the Middle Ages had little idea how the plague spread and it caused great fear and panic.

These herbs were used frequently in the Middle Ages. Wormwood (left) was put in clothes to get rid of fleas. Lemon balm (below left) was taken for fevers. Lungwort (below right) was used for chest disorders.

This well-ordered medieval herb garden must have been a source of many useful plants. Many of the plants usede in medieval times are still used today. For example, people thought that willow helped to cure headaches; modern aspirin comes from willow.

Many people were superstitious about herbs, and picked or used them on special days of the year.

Medieval people thought the root of the mandrake plant looked like a man, and it was even said that the plant shrieked when it was plucked. Mandrake was used as a sedative and pain-reliever.

30

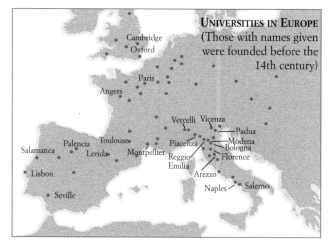

UNIVERSITIES IN EUROPE
(Those with names given were founded before the 14th century)

Medicine in the Middle Ages

In the Middle Ages there were few painkillers, so surgery was very painful. Surgical instruments were crude and were not sterilized. They were probably not even very clean, so there was a high risk of infection. Medieval doctors and patients were unaware of this problem.

Europe's first medical school was founded in Salerno, Italy, during the 800s. The later universities included medicine among their subjects. By the 14th and 15th centuries, universities had spread throughout Europe, as shown on the map. They made a great contribution toward the study of science and medicine. They also helped the sciences themselves to develop, as scholars came together and exchanged ideas.

A medieval surgeon operates on a patient's eye, to remove a cataract.

Universities

European universities developed from medieval cathedral and monastery schools. The first university opened in Bologna, Italy. It was founded in 1088 by a group of students who decided to employ scholars to teach them. In the following century, further universities were founded in Paris, France, and in Oxford and Cambridge, in England. The three main subjects taught during the Middle Ages were law, medicine, and religion.

Medieval students

This German miniature shows a group of students. The first German university was founded in Heidelberg in 1386. All universities charged fees, and if students were not happy and could afford to, they simply moved to another university. In 1209, for example, unhappy Oxford students moved to Cambridge. Twenty years later, many students moved from Paris to Oxford.

According to Ptolemy's system (above), the Sun, Moon, planets, and stars all moved around the Earth, which was at the center of everything. The solar system, with the Sun in the middle, was discovered by Copernicus in the 16th century.

Science and the Church

During the Middle Ages many scholars presented knowledge in a way that agreed with the Christian Church's view of the world. It was difficult for scientists and scholars to disagree openly with Christian ideas.

The Italian scholar Thomas Aquinas (c.1225–74) (left) was educated at a Benedictine school and later taught at the University of Paris. In his works and teachings, he tried to show that Christian faith and human reason can go well together and support each other. The Church declared Thomas Aquinas a saint in 1323.

A knight (left) is attended by maids as he takes a bath in a wooden tub. A servant is using bellows to keep a fire going to heat the water. People bathed far mess frequently during the Middle Ages. Knights usually only bathed before a special occasion, such as a feast or an important ceremony.

Medieval Islam

In the Middle Ages many Islamic scientists brought their knowledge together in large books. In the 11th century, for example, the Persian physician Avicenna (980–1037) wrote a medical encyclopedia, which showed how far advanced medicine was in the Arab world. His work was based on Arabic, Greek, and Roman medicine, and it became a popular text throughout the Middle East and Europe. The Muslims were skilled surgeons and mathematicians. They introduced the Arabic numeral system to Europe, as well as algebra.

The Muslim pharmacist (above) is preparing medicine over a fire.

Swedish Vikings rowed and sailed down the Dnieper, Volga, and other rivers in the 9th century. Viking ships were light, so they could be hauled or carried around rapids and across land when necessary. The Slavs who lived in the region of modern European Russia called the newcomers Varangians, and probably welcomed them as traders.

Among hunting peoples of the north, the brown bear was feared as a powerful, god-like symbol. Russian legends tell how the bear lived in heaven in the golden palace of the sky god. Some Russian peoples held a feast after a bear hunt. Guests had to bow to the dead bear and kiss its muzzle.

The battle helmet of Yaroslav I (980–1054), known as the Wise, who defeated his brother Svyatopolk to become grand prince of Kiev. Yaroslav founded Christian churches and monasteries, and employed scribes to translate Greek religious texts into the Slavic language. His three daughters married the kings of Norway, France, and Hungary.

Primary Chronicle

The Primary Chronicle is the earliest history of the birth of Russia. It was written in Kiev, probably in 1111. It states that Slavic groups in Novgorod quarreled and asked Viking traders to bring order to their land. One of the Viking leaders, named Rurik, settled in Novgorod and ruled the area around it. Historians are not sure that this story is true, since some of the Chronicle may have been based on legends, but it seems that the arrival of the Vikings was reasonably peaceful. The Chronicle goes on to say that another Varangian, called Oleg, took over Kiev in 882 and ruled as its prince. The ruler of Kiev was later given the title Grand Prince and ruled over other local leaders.

From the Baltic to the Black Sea

The Vikings' main waterway route ran from the Baltic Sea up the River Neva, through Lake Lagoda, up the River Volkhov to Novgorod, which had existed as a settlement since the 7th century. The Vikings went on south across Lake Ilmen, up the River Lovat, and then carried their ships to the headwaters of the Dnieper River, which flows for 1,420 miles – through modern Russia, Belarus, and Ukraine – to the Black Sea coast. The Dnieper passes through Kiev, which the Slavs had founded as early as the 5th century. Across the Black Sea lay Constantinople, which quickly became the main trading partner of the new Kievan state. Further east, the Vikings traveled all the way down the River Volga to the Caspian Sea.

According to a medieval chronicle, a group of related Varangian families settled in Holmgard (Novgorod) in 862, and the area became known as the "land of the Rus." This was the origin of modern "Russia." In the illustration (above), Slavs are offering a tribute of fur pelts to the Rus. Furs were an important trading product to the Vikings, who brought sable, ermine, and other valuable furs from the Arctic north. They also brought walrus ivory, as well as iron from their homelands.

Birth of Russia

The first Russian state was born in the 9th century when Swedish Vikings, known as Varangians, traveled south from the Baltic Sea. These explorers established and controlled trade routes along rivers and lakes all the way to the Black Sea. Furs, honey, and other forest products were taken across the Black Sea to Constantinople, where they were exchanged for silks, spices, and gold. The Vikings soon ruled the region, and integrated with the Slavic peoples who had lived there for hundreds of years. Kiev, the capital of modern Ukraine, developed as the most important city, and the region around it had its own prince. The other important region was to the north, around Novgorod. Kiev was influenced by the Byzantine Empire, and was converted to Christianity. In the 13th century, the first Russian state was overthrown by the Mongols.

The first two Russian saints, painted on a wooden icon. Saints Boris and Gleb were sons of Vladimir I (c.956–1015), who as grand prince of Kiev and Novgorod agreed with the Byzantine Emperor to become a Christian in 988. The two sons were killed by their brother, Svyatopolk the Accursed, who then seized power in Kiev.

This document (left) of 1147 was written in the Cyrillic alphabet. It makes the first known mention of Moscow, though a settlement had existed there since prehistoric times.

Miniature showing Vladimir I being baptized in 988. According to a medieval chronicle, Vladimir had decided that his state needed a major religion. He therefore sent envoys to report on Islam, Judaism, and Roman and Byzantine Christianity. He was won over by news of a magnificent mass held at Hagia Sophia cathedral in Constantinople. He also agreed to marry Anna, sister of the Byzantine Emperor Basil II. This was the start of the Russian Orthodox Church.

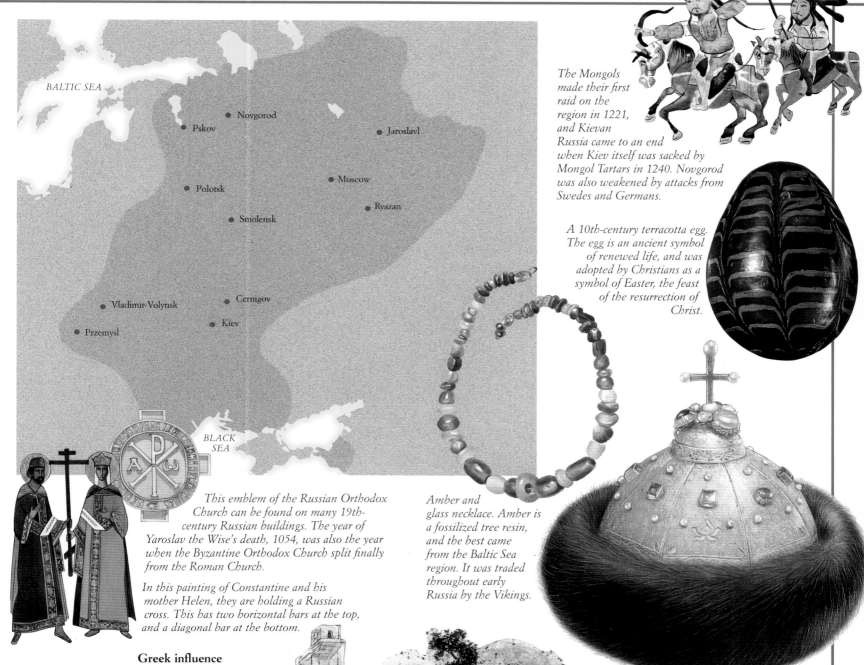

The Mongols made their first raid on the region in 1221, and Kievan Russia came to an end when Kiev itself was sacked by Mongol Tartars in 1240. Novgorod was also weakened by attacks from Swedes and Germans.

A 10th-century terracotta egg. The egg is an ancient symbol of renewed life, and was adopted by Christians as a symbol of Easter, the feast of the resurrection of Christ.

This emblem of the Russian Orthodox Church can be found on many 19th-century Russian buildings. The year of Yaroslav the Wise's death, 1054, was also the year when the Byzantine Orthodox Church split finally from the Roman Church.

In this painting of Constantine and his mother Helen, they are holding a Russian cross. This has two horizontal bars at the top, and a diagonal bar at the bottom.

Amber and glass necklace. Amber is a fossilized tree resin, and the best came from the Baltic Sea region. It was traded throughout early Russia by the Vikings.

The amazing Cap of State, a fur hat with precious metals and jewels that was first worn by Vladimir II (1053–1125), Grand Prince of Kiev, as a symbol of his power. Vladimir II was a strong ruler who fought many successful campaigns against Turkic invaders. He also founded new towns, including that of Vladimir, where the Cathedral of Saint Dimitrii was built later in the 12th century. Later Russian tsars inherited and wore Vladimir's Cap of State.

Saint Sophia cathedral, in Kiev, was named after Hagia Sophia in Constantinople. It was built by Yaroslav the Wise and dedicated by the first metropolitan bishop of Kiev in 1037.

Greek influence

Two Greek monks and missionaries translated the Christian scriptures into Slavic in the 9th century, which helped the Kievan people obtain both a religion and an alphabet. The two monks were brothers, who were later made saints: Cyril (c.827–69) and Methodius (c.825–84). The alphabet the brothers introduced was later called Cyrillic (after Saint Cyril) and is a modified Greek alphabet. It was originally made up of 43 letters, but modern versions have 30. After Cyril and Methodius, Christian missionaries from Constantinople continued to introduce the Cyrillic alphabet when they converted Russians, Serbs, Bulgars, and other Slavic peoples to Orthodox Christianity. Greek and Byzantine influence on the early Russians was considerable, in art and architecture as well as written language.

A Russian Orthodox priest carries an icon. These religious pictures, developed originally from Byzantine art, are important in many rituals of the Orthodox Church. They are carried at weddings and many other ceremonies, and are used instead of three-dimensional sculptures.

This icon is the masterpiece of the greatest Russian icon painter, Andrey Rublev (c.1370–1430). Entitled The Old Testament Trinity, the icon shows three angels who visited Abraham. The angels represent the three persons of the Christian God: Father, Son, and Holy Spirit. Rublev was influenced by Byzantine art, often worked with a famous Greek painter, and eventually became a monk.

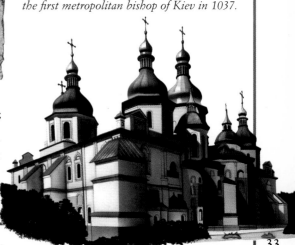

The German Empire and the Papacy

Charles the Bald was crowned Holy Roman Emperor by Pope John VIII on Christmas Day, 875. During his short reign some of the splendors of the age of Charlemagne were revived. His close links with the pope and the Church gave Charles great power.

When Otto the Great was crowned King of Germany in 936 and Holy Roman Emperor in 962, he brought the separate German duchies under the control of the monarchy. Under the Saxon emperors who followed him, the Holy Roman Empire was a powerful combination of territories. The next dynasty of German rulers, the Salians of Franconia, made strong emperors between 1024 and 1125. During their reigns, there was a series of disputes with popes. The main quarrel was about the right to appoint bishops, but there were wider problems. Neither the emperor nor the pope wanted to give power to the other, but they needed each other in order to have authority over all the people. When many German princes sided with the pope in the dispute, a series of civil wars broke out. It was the task of the next imperial dynasty, the Hohenstaufen of Swabia, to bring order back to the empire.

KINGDOM OF CHARLES THE BALD

KINGDOM OF LOUIS THE GERMAN

KINGDOM OF LOTHAIR I

After the death of Louis I, son of Charlemagne, civil war broke out in his empire. This was settled in 843, when the empire was divided between three of Louis' sons. Charles the Bald (823–77) received the western lands. Lothair took over the central territory, and Louis the German ruled in the east.

Hohenstaufen dynasty

The Hohenstaufens were a famous princely family of medieval Germany. They took their name from the ancestral castle built at Staufen in Swabia, southwest Germany, in the 11th century. The family's founder, Frederick of Hohenstaufen, received the duchy of Swabia from Emperor Henry IV in 1079 as a reward for loyal service, and he married Henry's daughter Agnes. His son, also called Frederick, claimed the right to the German crown, but in 1125 the German princes reaffirmed their right of free election. In 1138, the founder's grandson secured the German throne as Conrad III. Conrad's nephew, Frederick Barbarossa, succeeded him and became Holy Roman Emperor. Henry VI and Frederick II were further Hohenstaufen emperors, and the family held the imperial throne until 1254.

Otto III (980–1002) became Holy Roman Emperor at the age of three, so his mother and grandmother ruled until he was sixteen. He was the grandson of Otto the Great, who had driven invading Hungarians out of southern Germany and taken over the middle Frankish kingdom originally ruled by Lothair. His son, Otto II, successfully fought the Danes and Bohemians.

Above: Frederick I (c.1122–90), known as Barbarossa or "Red Beard," was a very popular German king of the Hohenstaufen dynasty, who became Holy Roman Emperor in 1155. He was unsuccessful in a bitter struggle with Pope Alexander III, and died on a crusade to the Holy Land. A famous legend says that Frederick never died, that his red beard still grows, and that he will one day return to rule Germany.

Left: A bust of Frederick II (1194–1250), who was called the "Wonder of the World" because he was such a brilliant ruler. He was crowned German king when he was two years old and became Holy Roman Emperor in 1215. He was a soldier and a scientist, but he also encouraged poets and artists.

St Michael's Church, in Hildesheim, Germany, was built between 1010 and 1033. The local bishop, Bernward, taught the German king, Otto III. The church is built in Ottonian style, named for the German kings.

One of Frederick II's falconers kneels before the emperor. Frederick was an expert huntsman. He wrote a book called On the Art of Hunting with Birds, which experts on falconry still refer to. Frederick liked to hunt near Castel del Monte in Italy.

Frederick II, the grandson of Barbarossa, built many castles throughout his empire. The most famous and best preserved is the Castel del Monte in the Puglia region of southern Italy. This massive Gothic castle was built in 1240, and its eight sides make it a perfect octagonal shape.

Investiture dispute

In 1075 Pope Gregory VII decided that only he should have the authority to appoint bishops. Before that time kings and emperors had done so, in return for pledges of loyalty. The king of Germany, Henry IV, disagreed with Gregory and declared that he was no longer pope. In turn, Gregory expelled Henry from the Church. Many German princes supported the pope, and Henry was forced to give in. But in 1084, the year that he was crowned Holy Roman Emperor, Henry captured Rome and replaced Gregory with another pope, Clement III. The struggle between pope and emperor did not end until 1122, when both Gregory and Henry were dead.

Henry IV is shown above, kneeling, with Matilda of Canossa and the Bishop of Cluny in 1077. It is said that when Henry reached Canossa, in Italy, he had to stand barefoot in the snow for three days while he waited for Pope Gregory VII to pardon him.

Pope Gregory IX (1148–1241) fought a long struggle against the power of the Holy Roman Empire. Gregory twice excommunicated Emperor Frederick II because he did not fulfil the vows that he had made.

The curved head of a bishop's staff, called a crosier. This ornate 11th-century example is made of ivory. A crosier is shaped like a shepherd's crook, and acted as a symbol of the way in which a bishop looked after his own flock – the people in his diocese, or district.

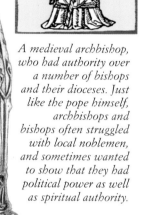

Emperor and pope are shown here (above) as the best of friends, helping and supporting each other on a joint throne. Unfortunately, the two leaders did not always get on this well in the Middle Ages, partly because of pressures from the nobles and bishops beneath them.

Papal power

Innocent III was elected pope in 1198, and he showed how powerful the office could be. He created an international court to hear appeals from throughout the Christian world, and he approved the first official collection of canons, or church laws. Innocent called himself the "Vicar of Christ," and he described the pope as being below God, but above all other people. In 1215, Innocent called one of the most important general councils of the Middle Ages, the Fourth Lateran Council, which met in Rome in 1215.

A medieval archbishop, who had authority over a number of bishops and their dioceses. Just like the pope himself, archbishops and bishops often struggled with local noblemen, and sometimes wanted to show that they had political power as well as spiritual authority.

A bishop's hat, called a "mitre," is a symbol of his office. In medieval times it represented his authority and power. This fine example was beautifully embroidered with gold thread and silk. Bishops usually came from noble families and were involved in affairs of state as well as church matters.

A miniature of a vision experienced by Hildegard of Bingen (1098–1179), a German abbess. Hildegard wrote about her visions, as well as her ideas on medicine and the lives of the Christian saints.

Innocent III (1160–1216) is thought of as the greatest of the medieval popes. He judged between rival emperors in Germany, supporting Frederick II against Otto IV in his bid for the imperial crown. Here, in a fresco by the Italian painter Giotto, Innocent dreams of St Francis of Assisi as a saviour of the Church.

This large gilt ring belonged to a medieval pope. The pope usually wears a papal ring, as well as a golden cross.

This medieval illustration shows a king officially appointing an abbot as the head of an abbey of monks. The pope and other church leaders were against this. They thought that only they had the authority to make religious appointments.

The coronation of Pope Clement V (1264–1314), who was appointed by the influence of King Philip IV of France. In 1309 Clement moved the papal court from Rome to Avignon, in southern France, where it remained until 1377.

The Feudal Kingdoms of France and England

In medieval Europe, kings divided their land among their most important noblemen. In return for the land, the nobles did homage to the king and became his vassals. They promised to serve the king and fight for him whenever they were needed. For this, they in turn required the service of knights, who were their vassals. We call this arrangement the feudal system, and it was particularly strong in France and England during the 12th and 13th centuries. Kings were at the head of strong central governments. They sometimes needed support for a particular plan, so they would call a meeting of nobles, bishops, knights, and townspeople. These meetings formed the beginning of parliaments, which made a country's laws. Nobles and others then had to try and make sure that their king would also obey the law.

THE KING
NOBLES, BISHOPS, LANDOWNERS
KNIGHTS, ABBOTS, CLERICS
PEASANTS, THE VERY POOR.

THE FEUDAL PYRAMID

In return for a grant of land, a nobleman pledged himself to his king and promised to be his faithful servant. In this way the nobleman, or lord, became the king's vassal, or retainer. The nobleman knelt in front of his king to swear his oath of loyalty.

Henry I (1068–1135), king of England and called "the Scholar," increased the power of the royal courts. In this miniature (left), Henry is shown suffering the nightmare of his country's peasants demanding more from him.

The English parliament developed in the 13th century, when kings consulted nobles and churchmen on important issues. In 1295, King Edward I widened the parliament by ordering two knights elected from each county and two representatives from each town to attend. This assembly was later called the Model Parliament and was the beginning of the British House of Commons, with elected members representing their constituents.

When King John (1167–1216) put his royal seal to the Magna Carta (or "Great Charter") in 1215, he agreed that he would keep to the laws of England, just like everyone else.

King John set his seal to the Magna Carta on June 15, 1215.

Edward I (1239–1307), who succeeded his father Henry III as king of England, conquered Wales and had a number of important castles built there. This classic concentric castle, at Beaumaris on the island of Anglesey, was built in 1295. It was well defended with two sets of surrounding walls and a moat.

Castles

A medieval castle was the fortified stronghold of a king or nobleman. If the castle was attacked, the drawbridge could be raised, so that there was no easy way to get across the surrounding moat. It was almost impossible to capture a castle except by siege, starving out a castle's defenders over a period of weeks or months. Over the centuries castles got bigger and stronger. Nobles and their families lived inside the main building, called the "keep," together with knights and servants. Concentric castles, such as this one (right), had more than one circle of walls around the keep, with battlements and towers along them. Defenders could shoot arrows from the towers.

This scene from the Bayeux Tapestry shows William I, the Conqueror, sitting on the throne as King of England. He was crowned king on Christmas Day, 1066, just ten weeks after King Harold had been killed at the Battle of Hastings.

The Domesday Book was produced in 1086, twenty years after the Norman conquest of England.

The Domesday Book

William the Conqueror ordered the production of the Domesday Book as a survey and record of the property holders of England. The king wanted to know how much land he owned, and the value of other land for tax purposes. Royal officers collected details of each manor, its owner, number of inhabitants, the services or rents they owed, as well as the number of plows, mills, and fisheries.

Richard II

Son of the Black Prince, a famous English warrior, Richard (1367–1400) came to the throne of England at the age of ten. During the early years of his reign, a council ruled England on his behalf. Later, Richard ruled on his own and became more and more tyrannical. He made a new law that everyone over the age of fifteen had to pay him a tax. This led to the famous Peasants' Revolt in 1381. In the 1390s he commissioned this portrait of himself (left) and had it placed in Westminster Abbey to remind everyone that he had been given his power by God. In 1399, Henry IV deposed him and Richard was locked in Pontefract Castle, where he died a year later.

A hunting scene from the Palace of the Normans in Palermo, Sicily.

The Normans in Sicily

The Normans conquered Sicily in the late 11th century, and Roger II became King of Sicily in 1130. His court was an important center for both Christian and Muslim scholars. By the end of the 12th century Sicily was the richest and most advanced state in Europe.

French kings carried a "hand of justice" to show that they controlled the law of the land.

Becket and his King

Thomas Becket was born about 1118, and in 1154 became King Henry II's chancellor. Eight years later Henry made Becket Archbishop of Canterbury, the most powerful English churchman. King Henry and the Archbishop began to argue over the power of the monarchy and the Church. Henry wanted his own set of laws and courts to rule, and when Becket disagreed, the king asked if no one would get rid of this "turbulent priest." Four knights slipped away from Henry's court and murdered Becket in Canterbury Cathedral. Three years later the Church declared him a saint.

Scene on a casket showing the murder of Thomas Becket.

A statue of the legendary Robin Hood.

Robin Hood

According to medieval legend, Robin Hood was an outlaw who lived with a band of loyal followers in Sherwood Forest, in central England. Robin and his "merry men" spent most of their time hunting the king's deer, practicing their archery skills, and robbing the rich to give to the poor. Robin's greatest enemy was the Sheriff of Nottingham, who was supposed to uphold the law in the county, but who was unjust and mistreated poor people. No one knows whether the legendary outlaw really existed, but he was first mentioned in stories in 1377.

ENGLAND AND FRANCE
IN 1300

Dublin

York

ENGLAND

Cambridge

London

Calais

Reims

Paris

Orléans

Bourges

Poitiers

FRANCE

Lyons

Bordeaux

Toulouse

In 1297 Philip IV (1268–1314), King of France (who called himself "the Fair" because he believed he was so good-looking, asked Edward I of England to visit him. Though they had been at war with each other, Edward was Philip's vassal because he was also the Duke of Aquitaine. Their long feud was settled when Edward's son married Philip's daughter in 1308.

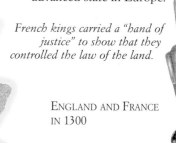

The Growth of Towns

Towns grew in size and importance throughout the Middle Ages, though most would still seem like large villages to us today. They were surrounded by protective walls and so could not grow beyond a certain size. Conditions within a town were certainly not comfortable, but there were good reasons why people went to live there. Many went to find work. Merchants settled in towns to start businesses where they had plenty of customers, and lawyers and bankers set up offices. Pedlars and traveling musicians journeyed between towns to earn their living. All these people needed food and clothing, so butchers, bakers, tailors, and shoemakers opened shops and were soon able to employ people too. As towns grew, mayors and councillors were appointed to govern them. Most people preferred this way of running things to the feudal system in the countryside, where people owed their loyalty to a local lord.

The seal of Conwy, in north Wales. This fortified town was founded by King Edward I of England in 1283 after he invaded Wales. Conwy Castle still stands, yet today the town has a population of little more than 13,000.

Trade associations, called guilds, were formed in medieval towns. Each trade or craft had its own guild, to fix prices and set standards of work. These are the emblems of the bakers' and tailors' guilds.

Medieval towns were very busy, with people coming and going to visit shops and especially the market. People from outside the town brought their wares to sell, and the narrow streets were full of pedlars. Town gates were opened at dawn and closed at dusk, and merchants often had to pay a toll to enter.

Learning a trade

It took a long time for a young person to learn a craft, and even longer to become a member of a guild. At the age of about seven, a boy might be taken on by a craftsman, such as this cooper, or barrel-maker (below), as an apprentice. At first the boy would watch how things were done and help with other tasks, such as fetching things and sweeping up the workshop. After seven years an apprentice became a journeyman, traveling to different towns and gaining experience from other masters. After several more years, the journeyman could present an example of his work, his "masterpiece," and join a guild if his work was good enough.

Chartres cathedral, in France, is famous for its 13th-century stained glass windows. This one shows fur merchants and drapers, whose guilds donated money for the cost of the window. Drapers sold textile fabrics.

This medieval butcher is portrayed in stained glass in Notre Dame cathedral, Paris. In the Middle Ages butchers and other shopkeepers had little idea of hygiene, and we would probably be horrified to see the state of their shops.

Towns could be dangerous places after dark. There was no street lighting, so nightwatchmen walked the streets with candlelit lanterns. Most people had to work very hard during the day, so they were happy to stay at home and sleep at night.

This 15th-century illustration (right) shows a lord being murdered in the street by a gang of three hired killers. Richer members of society usually made sure that they had strong servants with them.

Fire!

Rich town dwellers had houses made of stone or brick, but most people's houses were made of wood. The use of lanterns and candles in every home, as well as open fires for cooking, meant that the risk of fire was very high. Once a fire had started in a town, it spread very rapidly and was difficult to put out, since water was often not readily available. The city of Rouen, in France, burned to the ground six times between 1200 and 1225.

Criminals were tried in local courts, and punishment for those found guilty was usually harsh. Serious crimes were punishable by death, and execution was by hanging (right), beheading, or burning. Those convicted of less serious crimes might be dragged through the streets, whipped, or put in the stocks.

In the stocks

The punishments for small, petty crimes were usually intended to make offenders look silly. Women who gossiped too much were sometimes made to stand in a cart in the marketplace, where people could throw things at them. Others were put in the stocks. This was a wooden frame with holes for the legs of the victim, and sometimes also for the arms. People were put there for periods of a few hours to several days. Townspeople enjoyed pelting them with rubbish, rotten fruit, or even stones.

People accused of crimes were dealt with in a very public way. These two, shown in a 12th-century illustration, are being led through the streets naked. The trumpeters make sure that town dwellers gather to give the couple an uncomfortable, humiliating walk to court, prison, or even their execution.

Human waste was a great problem in medieval towns, since there was no proper method of sewage disposal. Some houses had a primitive outside lavatory. This illustration comes from a 15th-century edition of the Decameron by Giovanni Boccaccio (1313–75), a collection of stories told by young people who fled the plague-ridden streets of Florence in 1348.

Medieval towns were dirty and smelly. People threw their rubbish and emptied their pots out of windows onto the street. Town councils paid "scavengers" to collect refuse in carts and dump it outside the town walls. There were drainage ditches alongside some streets, and these became infested with rats. This caused disease to spread.

The most important European towns in the Middle Ages, with the year in which they were founded, and their medieval populations. Later, many of the towns became associated with a particular trade and grew in size. Others still exist today but are quite small.

Clocks

The first mechanical clocks were probably invented in China in the late 11th century. About 200 years later, Europeans had also developed weight-driven clocks that rang a bell every hour. This clock was made around 1390 and told the time in Wells Cathedral, England. During the day people used the sun to tell the time, but clocks such as this were particularly important at night, when the hourly bell told monks when to say their prayers. Dials and hour hands were added to clocks soon after this time.

This illustration was drawn in Constantinople, capital of the Byzantine Empire, in 1203. It shows the workings of a water pump. Medieval towns were in great need of fresh water as populations grew. Unless they had access to a well, most people took their water from the nearest river. Water sellers also brought fresh water in from outside the town.

EUROPEAN CITIES IN 1300
(Cities with more than 10,000 inhabitants)

INHABITANTS PER SQ.M
over 50
18–50
1–18

St Omer
Ypres
Bruges
Ghent
Utrecht
York
Lubeck
Danzig
Antwerp
Brunswick
Magdeburg
Bristol
London
Louvain
Cologne
Lille
1 2 3 4 5
Mainz
Rouen
Worms
Regensburg
Paris
Strasbourg
Brescia
Mantua
Piacenza
Verona
Milano
Padua
Bordeaux
Lyon
Pavia
Venice
Parma
Modena
Montpellier
Genoa
Bologna
Toulouse
Arles
Lucca
Forli
Albi
Pisa
Orvieto
Valladolid
Perpignan
Florence
Viterbo
Marseille
Siena
Rome
Naples
Zaragoza
Barcelona
Toledo
Valencia
Palma
Lisbon
Badajoz
Cordoba
Murcia
Palermo
Seville
Granada
Messina
Jerez
Almeria
Tunis
Catania
Cadiz
Malaga

1 Arras
2 Douai
3 Tournai
4 Brussels
5 Liege
6 Metz

MEDITERRANEAN SEA

Kaffa
Constantinople
Phocea
Aleppo
Antioch
Damascus
Jerusalem

Every important medieval town had its own seal. This seal of Limoges, in France, dates from 1303. Limoges was originally a Roman town and became a stopping place for pilgrims on the road to Santiago de Compostela (see page 25).

39

Medieval Architecture

A new style of architecture developed in Europe during the 10th century and flourished for the next 300 years or so. Historians call this style Romanesque because it was based on earlier Roman architecture, but it was also influenced by Carolingian and Byzantine styles. The most important Romanesque buildings were churches, which typically had thick walls, rows of columns built close together, curved arches, and small windows. As building skills advanced, medieval masons were able to build taller, more graceful churches. By the 12th century, a new style had developed, which we call Gothic. The new Gothic cathedrals had thinner, taller walls with high windows, arches, and towers, and they were decorated with beautiful stained glass, carvings, and sculpture. This style was so successful that Gothic churches and other structures were built right through to the end of the Middle Ages.

Builders put up wooden scaffolding for stonemasons to work on. Heavy stones were lifted up to them on a windlass, or hoist, which was worked by a large wooden treadmill.

Building a Gothic cathedral
Hundreds of medieval masons and carpenters were involved in building a cathedral, and it usually took several years to complete. A master mason planned the building and watched over all the workers. Wooden scaffolding was used both for the builders and as a framework for some of the stone construction. Masons cut blocks of building stone, carriers hauled up the materials, and experienced freemasons fitted the stones in place, and carved decorative moldings.

The devilish figure (above) acts as a spout, called a "gargoyle," to carry rainwater from the roof and clear of the walls of the Cathedral of Notre Dame, in Paris. Grotesque gargoyles were common on Gothic buildings, such as Notre Dame, which was built in 1163–1250.

Cutting and shaping stone was skilled work. Masons used a strong iron chisel (left) and a wooden mallet. Triangular dividers helped them compare measurements and mark out curves.

The abbess Uta, and teacher and monk Ekkehart (below), were sculpted as founders of the cathedral at Naumburg.

In the 13th century, most sculptors' work was for cathedrals and churches.

Spire, tallest part of the cathedral

Pitched roof

Wooden centering, or framework

Pinnacle

Tall, narrow Gothic window

Pointed arch

Gargoyle (water spout)

Parapet

Buttress

Flying buttress strengthens the wall

Wooden scaffolding

Art and sculpture

Because the windows of Romanesque churches were small, there was a lot of wall space for decoration. This was mostly taken up with frescoes, or wall paintings, which illustrated Bible stories, but few of these survive today. Most Romanesque sculpture was done in relief, which meant it was carved from a background of stone. By the 12th century statues were beginning to look more lifelike, and the Gothic style developed this still further. Gothic figures were longer and more graceful, and many beautiful ones were carved on the columns and doors of religious buildings.

The group of buildings in the Square of Miracles in Pisa was constructed over more than 200 years. The cross-shaped Romanesque cathedral was begun in 1063; the round baptistery and bell tower were founded in the 12th century; and the cemetery followed a century later. All were built of white marble. The bell tower is the famous Leaning Tower of Pisa, which started tilting as soon as it was built and today leans more than 16 feet from the vertical.

This bas-relief of Eve was carved in the 12th century by an artist called Gislebertus. He also did many sculptures for Autun Cathedral, in France. Many have been kept in excellent condition because they were plastered over in the 18th century and forgotten.

The Norman church at Kilpeck, in England, dates from about 1140 – less than a hundred years after the Norman conquest of the country. The highly decorated south doorway shows a style which today's experts call High Romanesque.

The cathedral at Burgos, in Spain, was founded in 1221. The ornate Gothic towers were added in the 15th century.

Stained-glass windows were a favorite way to decorate medieval churches. They are like mosaics, using small pieces of colored glass held together by lead strips. The pictures usually tell stories from the Bible, which seem to come to life as light streams through the window. The earliest surviving windows date from the 12th century. Chartres Cathedral, in France, is famous for its 13th-century stained glass and contains more than 150 windows.

This relief (below) was carved over the doorway of a church in Arles, France, in the 12th century. It shows Christ surrounded by symbols of Matthew, Mark, Luke, and John.

This scene of the Three Kings bringing gifts to baby Jesus is part of a row of 6th-century mosaics in the Sant'Apollinare Nuovo church in Ravenna, Italy.

Stained-glass window

From the 14th century more effort and money were put into civic buildings such as guild halls and town halls. The Town Hall of medieval Bamberg, Germany, was built in 1453 on an island in the river that flows through the town. The "bishop's town" was on one side of the river, and the "people's town" on the other.

MAJOR GOTHIC CATHEDRALS

1 Wells
2 Salisbury
3 Winchester
4 Chichester
5 Rouen
6 Beauvais
7 Paris

8 Senlis
9 Soissons
10 Chartres
11 Sens
12 Troyes
13 Orléans
14 Auxerre
15 Dijon
16 Bourges

Main centers of Romanesque art
Area of origin of Gothic art

Gothic architecture

Gothic architecture started in France with the abbey church of St Denis in 1137, followed by the cathedral of Notre Dame in 1163. But the term Gothic was only used hundreds of years later, and it was originally meant as a term of disapproval by artists who wanted to return to a simpler, classical style.

Bodiam Castle, in England, was put up in 1385 to defend against a possible French invasion. It was built with high solid walls surrounded by a wide moat, with a quadrangular court inside.

In this relief, the people of Milan return to their city after it was captured by the German Holy Roman Emperor, Frederick Barbarossa, in 1162.

Lombard League

In 1167 the pope supported the cities of Lombardy, such as Milan, Cremona, and Pavia, when they formed a league to support each other. They fought against domination by the Holy Roman Emperor, Frederick Barbarossa. In 1176 the League defeated Frederick's army at Legnano, and he was forced to accept the freedom of the city states.

MAIN CITIES IN 12TH–13TH CENTURY ITALY

Como
Legnano
Bergamo
Verona
Venice
Milan
Crema
Pavia
Lodi
Mantua
Alessandria
Genoa
Bologna
Lucca
Florence
Pisa
Arezzo
Siena
Perugia
Chieti
ADRIATIC SEA
Aquila
Rome
Montecassino
Barletta
Benevento
Trani
Gaeta
Melfi
Naples
Salerno
Taranto
Brindisi
Amalfi
Potenza
Castrovillari
TYRRNENIAN SEA
Cosenza
Crotone
Cagliari
IONIAN SEA
Palermo
Cefalù
Messina
Reggio
Catania

Italian City States

From the beginning of the 11th century, cities in northern Italy grew rapidly in size and importance. They became centers of trade and banking, and the wealthiest developed into independent city states. The largest and most influential were Florence, Milan, and Venice, but there were many others. These new states controlled the farming lands outside their city walls, but they often quarreled and fought against each other. There were violent disagreements within the cities too. The clearest division was between the parties of the Guelphs and the Ghibellines. The Guelphs supported supreme rule by the pope, while the Ghibellines favored the overall power of the emperor. Cities traditionally supported one faction or the other, and this led to further disagreements, which weakened the city states. Nevertheless, the cities helped toward the great cultural blossoming of the Renaissance, which began in Italy in the 14th century.

In the 13th century, the nobleman and Ghibelline leader Farinata degli Uberti (above) saved Florence from complete destruction after his party had defeated the Florentine Guelphs.

The leader of the Sienese army, Guidoriccio da Fogliano, was a mercenary, or hired soldier. City states used mercenaries, many of them foreign soldiers, to fight their battles. The leaders were ruthless businessmen who made a lot of money out of war. Some of them later began to conquer territories for themselves.

Around the year 1200 Florence had about 30,000 inhabitants, but a century later the number had risen to 100,000. Florentine workers developed new ways of refining wool, while successful bankers brought great wealth to the city.

The famous gold florin was first made in Florence in 1252. It became important currency for trade throughout Europe. The lily was the symbol of Florence. On the other side of the coin was a figure of Saint John the Baptist, the city's patron saint.

Merchants and bankers brought great wealth to the Italian city states, especially to Florence.

This "lion's mouth" stood in the meeting room of Venice's powerful Council of Ten. Secret accusations against people could be posted through the mouth.

The "doge," or leader, of Venice wore an unusual hat woven in gold and silver cloth. The doge was elected from among the richest and most powerful Venetian families. After 1032 the city's people limited the doge's power by surrounding him with officials.

Genoa and Venice

The city of Genoa was an important port and naval state, like Venice. During the 12th century Genoa made strong trading links with places as far away as Constantinople, Syria, and Tunis. At the height of the city's power a century later, it controlled the central Mediterranean, including the islands of Corsica and Sardinia. There was a series of wars with the rival city of Venice, and the Venetians finally defeated the Genoese in 1380.

Council of Ten

In 1310 Venice created a Council of Ten to protect the security of the city. These ten powerful men met in the Doges' Palace to decide on the fate of serious offenders. A door from their meeting room led to the State Inquisitor's room, from where offenders could be taken to the prison or, even worse, the torture chamber.

The original Doges' Palace in Venice was destroyed by an uprising in 976. A new residence for the city's ruler was built in the early 14th century.

The textile market in Bologna was full of workshops, shops, and merchants. In the Middle Ages Bologna had 180 towers, of which two 12th-century examples still stand today.

A medieval Venetian ducat. Merchants from Venice traded throughout the Mediterranean and made it a very rich city.

Craftsmen and workers receiving payment for their services to the city of Siena.

The tower of the Palazzo Pubblico, in Siena, was finished in 1348. It is 285 feet high and was built as a symbol of the city's power.

The large illustration below is based on a fresco in the Siena Town Hall called The Effects of Good and Bad Government, painted by Ambrogio Lorenzetti in 1338–9.

Merchants and Bankers

By the 12th century, merchants were traveling long distances along trade routes that linked the growing European cities. Luxury goods began to arrive from Asia and Africa, and cargo ships carried them from the great Italian ports of Venice and Genoa to the towns of northern Europe. Italian merchant companies were the first to operate as banks by issuing notes of credit and lending money to traders. This meant that merchants no longer had to carry all their valuables with them and risk being robbed. In the big towns and cities, trade associations, called guilds were formed. Each trade or craft had its own guild, to fix prices and set standards of work, and to make sure that outsiders could not compete. Supported by the bankers, who themselves became rich from their trade, medieval merchants spread across Europe.

The magnetic compass made navigation much easier for sailors. A simple version was first used by Chinese and Mediterranean sailors in about 1100. In the 1300s the standard compass was marked off into 32 points of direction.

Trade routes

The map shows the most important commercial centers, trading products, and traveling routes in medieval Europe. Most journeys along the trade routes took a long time. From Venice, for example, a journey to London normally took 4 weeks, to Lisbon 7 weeks, and to Damascus 12 weeks. Luxury goods such as silk, jade, and porcelain took even longer to come overland all the way from China, while spices were brought by ship from Southeast Asia. Gold from Africa was carried by Arab merchants across the vast sands of the Sahara Desert. The trading cities grew quickly as regular fairs and markets were set up by the merchants.

The sculpture of a winged lion is from a palace in Venice, the most important port in medieval Europe. It is the lion of Saint Mark, the patron saint of the city.

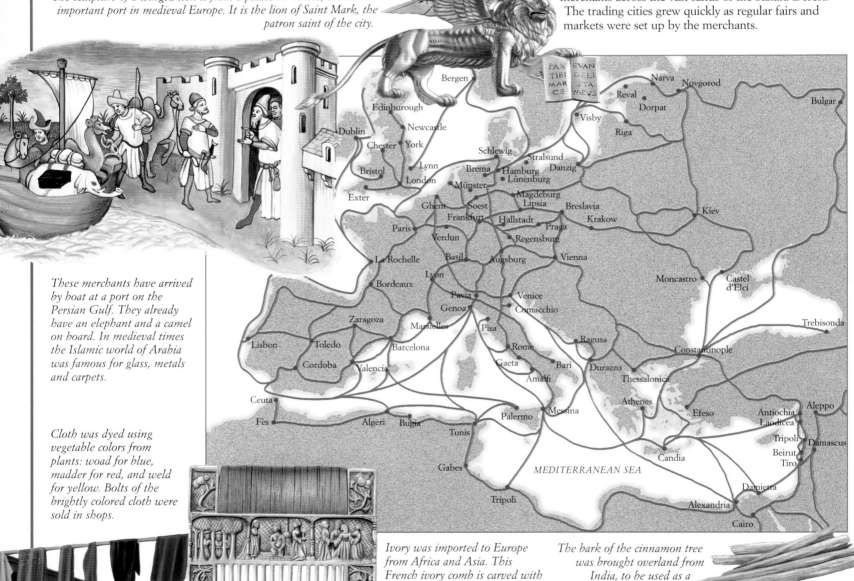

These merchants have arrived by boat at a port on the Persian Gulf. They already have an elephant and a camel on board. In medieval times the Islamic world of Arabia was famous for glass, metals and carpets.

Cloth was dyed using vegetable colors from plants: woad for blue, madder for red, and weld for yellow. Bolts of the brightly colored cloth were sold in shops.

Ivory was imported to Europe from Africa and Asia. This French ivory comb is carved with the History of Susanna *from the Old Testament of the Bible.*

The bark of the cinnamon tree was brought overland from India, to be used as a fragrant spice. The bark was dried and rolled, to make cinnamon sticks.

These Chinese ladies are ironing a newly woven length of silk. Silk was discovered in ancient China, probably thousands of years before it ever came to Europe. In the Middle Ages, it was a most important trading product.

Hand-held scales were also used to weigh produce. Medieval people were very aware of the value of all kinds of goods, including food. Any baker found guilty of selling bread short in weight might be dragged through the streets with a loaf of bread tied around his neck.

The city of Hamburg grew up around the Hammaburg castle in about 825. Standing between the Alster and Elbe rivers it has a good natural port. A founding member of the Hanseatic League, Hamburg was an important center of trade throughout the Middle Ages.

The silver coin (below) was minted in Trento, Italy, around 1180. The later gold coin (above) is also Italian. The first gold coins since Roman times were minted in Florence in the 13th century.

The seal of the city of Kiel, on the north German coast, shows a typical Hanseatic trading ship. This particular seal was used to stamp a document in 1436.

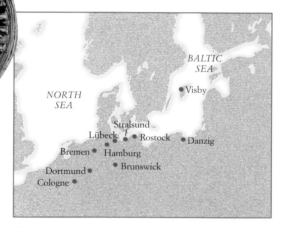

This map shows the main cities in the Hanseatic League, as well as other important trading cities.

Merchants and bankers used small portable scales to weigh coins, which were mostly made of silver. The weight of the metal was used to determine the coins' value, so it was easy to compare different currencies and difficult for anyone to cheat.

The Hanseatic League

In the 13th century trading cities along the North Sea and Baltic coasts started to band together to protect their common interests. The port of Hamburg was an important member of this Hanseatic League, or Hansa (which comes from an Old German word meaning "company"). By the middle 1300s, the League included all the larger German cities, and by 1400 it had members in 160 towns in northern Europe. Meetings were held at Lübeck, where members discussed how to help each other gain control of foreign trade and fight pirates and bandits. If a town refused to join the League, the merchants of that town found it impossible to sell their goods in profitable markets. The League gained control of the fur trade with Russia, the fish trade with Norway and Sweden, and the wool trade with Belgium. Members also developed a system of commercial laws, to protect themselves against others. The Hansa lasted as a powerful force until 1669.

Italian moneychangers sat at a long, narrow table, or "banca," which is where the word bank comes from.

Typical merchants' houses in the city of Bruges, Belgium, which was one of the most important trading cities in Europe between 1250 and 1500. Merchants in Bruges traded with the Hanseatic League and Venice, and by 1450 the city had a population of almost 100,000 people. Today, Bruges is still known for its lace and textiles.

Spices were brought from Asia by land and sea. This illustration shows berries being harvested from pepper vines, somewhere in southern Asia. The berries were dried to make the peppercorns that we still buy today.

The Mongol Empire

The Mongols were a community of tribes, or family clans, living scattered across the wide open grasslands of central Asia, where Mongolia, China, and Russia are today. They were nomadic peoples, moving their tents and possessions in carts from one campsite to the next. They herded flocks of sheep and goats with them in a never-ending search for new pastures. In the early years of the 1200s, the Mongol tribes were united under a single, powerful leader – Genghis Khan. He began the formation of the Mongol Empire by taking the lands of nearby kingdoms. Genghis Khan and his descendants ruled over the largest empire that the world has ever seen for almost 200 years. But this huge empire proved hard to control, and during the 1400s it broke up into its many parts.

In 1206, a 39-year-old Mongol called Temuchin was chosen as the ruler, or "khan," of the Mongols. He took the name Genghis, or Supreme Ruler. Genghis Khan (1167–1227) vowed to conquer the world and within a few years his vast empire covered Asia and beyond.

Empire of the Mongols
The armies of Genghis Khan and the leaders who came after him swept outward from the plains of central Asia to invade the lands of their neighbors. At its greatest extent, the empire of the Mongols stretched from Korea in the east to Poland in the west, and from the Arctic in the north to Persia in the south. No other empire – ancient or modern – has ever controlled so much land.

The success of the Mongols had much to do with their knowledge of horses, and their skill in riding them. Horses were fast and could travel long distances. In battle, the cavalry used speed and surprise to overcome the enemy. Mongol soldiers fought with bows and arrows, and with lances.

Kublai Khan (c.1216–94) was the grandson of Genghis Khan. He was a statesman and warrior, and under his leadership the Mongols conquered much of China. Kublai moved his capital to Beijing, where he established himself as emperor – the first outsider ever to rule over China. He built roads, gave food to the poor, and cared for the sick.

These elegantly decorated stirrups were made specially for the first Mongol leader, Genghis Khan.

A bronze disk bearing a message was issued to a person traveling on official business. It acted like a passport, granting the person permission to move around the land. Even people who could not read it knew what it was just by looking at it.

Mongol saddles were made from wood. They were highly prized and were often decorated.

Each time they moved to a new campsite, the Mongols brought their tents, called yurts, with them. A thick layer of felt made from sheep's wool was rolled over a wicker frame. Canvas sheets were tied over the felt. The door faced south, away from the wind.

In the 1260s, two merchants, Niccolo and Maffeo Polo, from Venice, Italy, began to trade with the Mongols. The brothers visited Kublai Khan: he was as curious about them as they were about him. It might have been during this encounter that Kublai Khan heard about Christianity, for he gave the Polos letters to hand to the pope, asking him to send 100 wise men.

KHANATE OF THE GOLDEN HORDE

BLACK SEA

CASPIAN SEA

CHAGATAI KHANATE

THE GREAT KHANATE

JAPAN

MEDITERRANEAN SEA

ILKHANATE

ARABIA

ARABIAN OCEAN

SULTANATE OF DEHLI

GULF OF BENGAL

Charging into battle, a group of Mongol cavalrymen attack their enemy at close range with steel axes, swords, and lances. These warriors are also armed with bows and arrows, for long-range fighting. In hand-to-hand combat they used wicker shields to deflect blows, while leather armor and iron helmets protected their bodies.

The arts, such as the theater, flourished in China under the Mongol rulers. Theaters were built in towns and cities. Actors, like the man shown in this clay model, sang, danced, and performed plays to entertain audiences. Popular dramas featured stories set in courtrooms – they could be funny or sad.

The best-quality Mongol clothes, such as this tunic worn by a man during the 1300s, were made from silk. Silk making had been practiced in China for thousands of years, and the process was a closely guarded secret. Cocoons of silkworm caterpillars were unraveled and the strands of silk were wound onto wooden frames. The strands were so fine that several were twisted together to make a single thread strong enough to weave on a loom.

One of the great discoveries of the Chinese was porcelain. As early as the AD 600s, potters mixed kaolin, a fine clay, with feldspar, a mineral, from which they made their pots. When heated very hot the ingredients fused together to make a hard, white material with a glassy surface. European potters did not learn how to make porcelain until the 1700s.

For centuries, the Mongols had written in a script called Uigur. But as their empire expanded into new lands, Uigur was not understood in them. Kublai Khan attempted to solve the problem by introducing one script for everyone. The script, called Phags-pa after its Tibetan inventor, is seen here, carved on a wooden seal.

47

The Reconquista

In the early 700s the Moors – Arabs, Berbers, and other Muslim peoples from northern Africa – invaded and occupied Spain. By the 11th century the different groups of Moors were fighting with each other and their territory split into many small Muslim states. Groups of Christians in northern Spain had remained independent, and they took the opportunity to expand their kingdoms southward, driving the Moors toward the Mediterranean Sea. Castile became the strongest of the Spanish kingdoms, and its soldiers led the fight against the Moors. By the 13th century Portugal controlled its present-day territory, and soon afterward Muslim-controlled land was reduced to the Kingdom of Granada in the very south of Spain. The Moors held their last stronghold there for a further 200 years, until the kingdoms of Castile and Aragon came together to unite Spain and drive out the Muslims. In 1492 the reconquest of Spain was complete.

The Nasrids
Nasrid leaders ruled Granada from 1238 to 1492. The first Nasrid ruler, Muhammad al-Ghalib, was a vassal of King Ferdinand III of Castile, but he made Granada rich and strong by welcoming Muslim refugees from the reconquered territories of Seville, Valencia, and Murcia.

This huge vase (left) dates from the time of the Nasrid dynasty in Granada, the last of the Muslim dynasties in Spain.

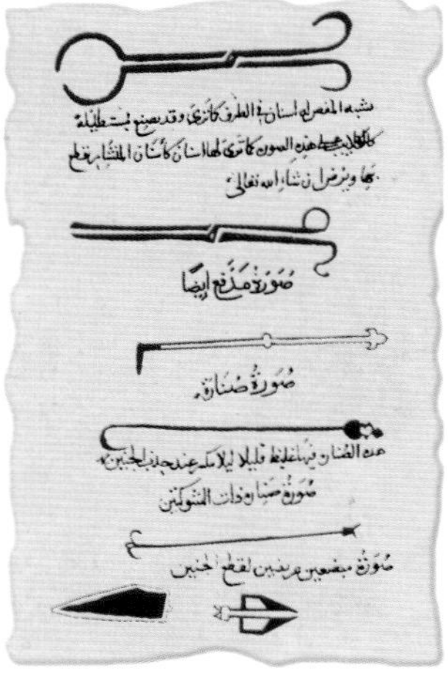

At their court in Cordoba, the Muslim caliphs (rulers) brought together the most important scholars. By the 10th century the library of Caliph al-Hakan had 400,000 books. This manuscript (right) shows surgical instruments.

The city of Cordoba was taken by the Moors in 711 and became their capital in 756. Nine years later they built the Great Mosque there, which is famous for its wonderful Moorish architecture (left). Cordoba silks, leatherwork, and jewelry were prized throughout Europe.

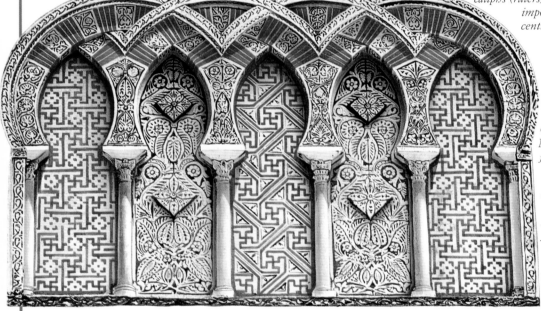

The Court of the Lions (below) is one of many beautiful courtyards and gardens within the citadel of the Alhambra, which stands above the city of Granada. The citadel had the Arabic name Al-Qal'a al-Hambra, meaning "the Red Fort," for the color of the sun-dried bricks that made up its outer walls. Though originally built as a military fortress, the Alhambra was developed into a beautiful palace, especially during the reign of King Yusuf I (1333–54). Its courtyards are surrounded by shady arcades and terraces, and the restored palace is a popular tourist attraction today.

The last Moorish stronghold
At Granada Moorish warriors built a fortress on the remains of an ancient stronghold called Alcazaba. They strengthened the original fortress with high walls, towers, and ramparts. This became the famous citadel of Alhambra, which contained houses, shops, mosques, public baths, a prison, and a hospital, as well as a palace. As the Moors were forced to retreat farther and farther toward the Mediterranean coast, King Muhammad XI withdrew to his safest stronghold. But the Spanish forces were too powerful, and on January 2, 1492 Muhammad was forced to surrender the entire city of Granada. Muslim rule in Spain was over.

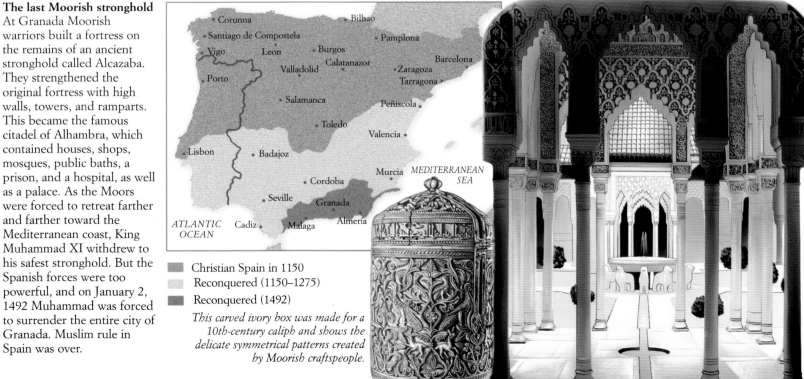

- ▇ Christian Spain in 1150
- ▢ Reconquered (1150–1275)
- ▇ Reconquered (1492)

This carved ivory box was made for a 10th-century caliph and shows the delicate symmetrical patterns created by Moorish craftspeople.

Map labels: Corunna, Bilbao, Santiago de Compostela, Pamplona, Vigo, Leon, Burgos, Barcelona, Valladolid, Calatanazor, Zaragoza, Tarragona, Porto, Salamanca, Peñiscola, Toledo, Valencia, Lisbon, Badajoz, Murcia, MEDITERRANEAN SEA, Cordoba, Seville, Granada, ATLANTIC OCEAN, Cadiz, Malaga, Almería

El Cid

Rodrigo Díaz de Vivar (c.1043–99) served in the army of the King of Castile. In 1081 he was banished by King Alphonso VI after being wrongly accused of disloyalty. Díaz then gathered together his own small army and after successful battles became rich and powerful. He was known as El Cid, from an Arabic word meaning "lord." In 1094, he defeated the Moors and conquered Valencia.

This statue of El Cid (above) stands in the Castilian city of Burgos, where he is buried.

This statue (left) shows one of the most important medieval Muslim philosophers, who spent most of his life in Cordoba. Averroes (1126–98), whose Arabic name was Ibn Rushd, was a physician and a judge, but he is most famous for his books on the ancient Greek philosophers Aristotle and Plato. Averroes' commentaries had a great influence on Christians and Jews, as well as on Muslims. He defended philosophy as the highest form of human thought, saying that religious faith and reason did not conflict with each other. Averroes believed that they were simply different ways of arriving at the truth.

Alcazar

As they battled to reconquer their lands, the Castilians and others built strong fortresses to defend themselves against the Moors. Each of these is called an alcazar, from the Arabic for fortress, and the most famous are at the cities of Segovia (recaptured in 1079), Toledo (recaptured in 1085), and Seville (recaptured in 1248). The Segovia alcazar (left) was first built in the 11th century and served its purpose throughout the Middle Ages. It was largely destroyed by fire in 1862, but has since been restored.

Scholars and poets enjoy the garden of Hisdai ibn Shaprut (c.915–75), a Jewish physician who acted as counselor to the Muslim caliph of Cordoba.

Castile and Aragon

The marriage of Ferdinand of Aragon (1452–1516) and Isabella of Castile (1451–1504) united the two largest Spanish kingdoms. Isabella was a strong queen who gained the support of the nobles in her kingdom. Ferdinand was a good military leader, who also brought peace and stability to Aragon. When the two kingdoms joined forces, it marked a turning point in Spain's history. The Moors were soon driven out, and King Ferdinand and Queen Isabella saw that their children married heirs of other kingdoms, so that Spain gained powerful allies throughout Europe.

In 1479 Ferdinand (left) became king of Aragon. His wife, Isabella (right), was already queen of Castile.

The Spanish Inquisition

In 1478 Pope Sixtus IV set up an Inquisition in Spain, which meant that people could be investigated to find out if they followed the teachings of the Roman Catholic Church. If they did not, they were called heretics. Many Muslims and Jews, even those who had supposedly converted to Christianity, were forced to leave Spain, while others were tortured or killed. King Ferdinand and Queen Isabella used the Inquisition to enforce loyalty to the crown as well as to the Church.

The seal of Alfonso Henriques (1110–85), known as "the Conqueror," who was the first king of Portugal. In 1139 Alfonso gained his new country's independence from the Spanish kingdom of Leon, and eight years later he drove the Muslims from Lisbon.

The Almohads

The Almohads were Moorish Muslims who ruled much of north Africa and Spain from 1130. Alfonso VIII (1155–1214), the King of Castile, fought against the Almohad invaders for many years and was badly defeated in 1195. However, Alfonso managed to get support from the neighboring Spanish kingdoms of Aragon, Leon, and Navarre, and in 1212 he won a great victory over the Almohad sultan at Las Navas de Tolosa, capturing the Almohad flag (above). The Almohads retreated to their north African provinces.

Those found guilty of heresy by the courts of the Spanish Inquisition were dealt with very harshly. They were tortured and often killed. Their property was taken by the court and shared between the inquisitors, the royal court, and their accusers. This encouraged people to accuse Muslims and Jews.

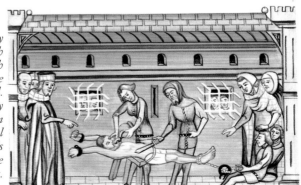

The Hundred Years War

From time of the Norman Conquest of 1066, English kings had ruled over lands in both England and France. At one point, more than half of France had been ruled by England, but by the time of Edward III (reigned 1327–77) only the southern wine-making provinces of Gascony and Guienne were in English hands – and it was only a matter of time before these too were lost. To retain his French territories, Edward declared war on France in 1337, and so began a long series of raids and invasions, with intervals of peace in between. Known as the "Hundred Years War," the fortunes of both sides were up and down. The English won important battles at Crécy (1346), Poitiers (1356), and Agincourt (1415), but when Joan of Arc – a teenage French girl – saved Orléans in 1429, the tide turned in favor of France. By 1453 the English had been driven out and the war was finally over.

Trade wars
The English fought the war to extend their territory in France, and to protect their businesses in Europe. English wool was exported, and French wine was imported. If these money making businesses were lost, English traders would suffer.

A gold coin struck in the reign of Edward III to commemorate his victory over the French at the sea battle of Sluys (1340), hence the image of the ship. Edward was the first English monarch to issue gold coins.

To show his claim to be the rightful king of France, as well as king of England, Edward III changed the English royal coat of arms. He produced a new design in which the fleurs-de-lis (lilies) of France were combined with the lions of England. His troops went into battle with this pattern on their flags, shields, and armor.

Calais 1347: Edward III's secret weapon
Calais, a port on the north coast of France, was besieged by Edward III's army in 1347. During the long siege, the English used a secret weapon against the French – the cannon. For the first time in Europe, gunpowder was used to fire lead balls and arrows at an enemy. Calais was taken and the town became the main landing point in France for English troops.

The first major battle of the Hundred Years War took place at sea, near the port of Sluys, in Flanders.

The sea battle of Sluys
In 1340, an English fleet of some 180 ships, carrying 4,000 infantry and 12,000 archers, was about to land when a large fleet of French ships was sighted. The English, with the wind and tide on their side, attacked the French ships, many of which were at anchor and made easy targets. Victory in the battle of Sluys (left) gave the English control of the Channel. This meant that English troops could cross the sea between England and France without danger of attack.

Agincourt
In 1415, Henry V's army of 6,000 troops faced a 20,000-strong French army at Agincourt (above). When French knights on horseback attacked, Henry's bowmen drove them back with their deadly arrows. Then they attacked the French foot-soldiers with swords. It was a famous English victory, and Henry was its hero.

Edward's tomb is in Canterbury Cathedral.

The Black Prince
Edward III had six sons and five daughters. His eldest son, Edward (1330–76) was known as the "Black Prince," since he went into battle wearing black armor. This warrior prince, who had fought at Crécy, died before becoming king.

Jacques Coeur, a wealthy Burgundian merchant banker.

Burgundy
Burgundy, a region in central France, was a wealthy and prosperous area that both sides wished to control. When the Duke of Burgundy switched sides and went over to the English, Henry V's French territory increased in size. But in 1435, as the English began to lose control of towns and cities, the Duke went back to the French side, and England's position was further weakened.

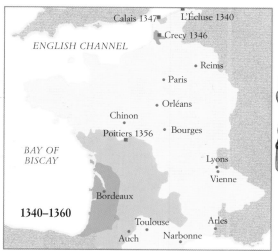

1340–1360

Calais 1347   L'Écluse 1340
Crecy 1346
ENGLISH CHANNEL
Reims
Paris
Orléans
Chinon
Poitiers 1356   Bourges
Lyons
Vienne
BAY OF BISCAY
Bordeaux
Toulouse   Arles
Auch   Narbonne

1340–1360

▢ Kingdom of France

▢ Territories passed to Edward III in 1360

▢ Territories acquired by Edward III in 1327

▪ English victories

The areas gained by England during the long war with France. When the war ended in 1453, all that the English had gained had been taken back by the French – with the exception of the port of Calais on the northern coast. This town remained an English possession until 1558.

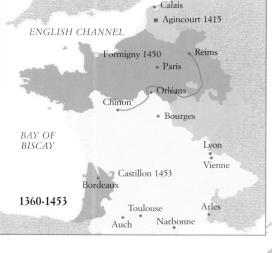

1360-1453

Calais
Agincourt 1415
ENGLISH CHANNEL
Formigny 1450   Reims
Paris
Orléans
Chinon
Bourges
BAY OF BISCAY
Lyon
Vienne
Castillon 1453
Bordeaux
Toulouse   Arles
Auch   Narbonne

1360-1453

▢ Kingdom of France

▢ Burgundian territories acknowledging Henry VI

▢ Territories annexed by henry VI in 1429

▢ Calais

→ Joan's of Arc itinerary

▪ French Victories

▪ English Victories

The social consequences of war
It was the ordinary people of France and England who had to pay for the war. Their governments imposed taxes on them, which the poor found difficult – if not impossible – to pay. There were protests against the new taxes, and riots broke out. In this illustration (above), drawn in the early 1300s, rioters are shown ransacking the house of a wealthy merchant in Paris.

Like many towns of the Middle Ages, Orléans was fortified with a strong wall. But when it fell to a French army in 1429, the English presence in France began to weaken.

Joan of Arc (c.1412–31) said that the saints had spoken to her, telling her to rescue France. She helped take Orléans from the English, but two years later, in 1431, she was captured and burned as a witch.

The house at Donrémy in which Joan of Arc was born still stands. Joan was the daughter of poor farmers, whose sheep she looked after on the hillsides near her home.

Charles VII of France (reigned 1422–61) is also known as Charles the Victorious. It was during this king's reign that France regained much of her land from the English.

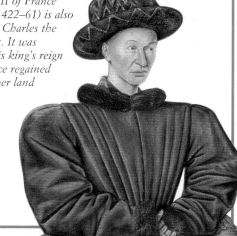

Knights and Warfare

Medieval noblemen divided their land among the knights who were trained to fight on horseback and win their battles for them. At the same time knights swore to uphold the noble code of chivalry by serving their king, the Church and their lady, as well as their lord. Not all knights observed these rules, however, and gallant behavior probably occurred more often in medieval romances than in real life. Knights were the most powerful men in society, and weaker men had to put themselves under their protection. Warfare was a knight's way of life, and his fighting skill was more important than anything else. To keep in practice for battle, knights took part in tournaments and challenged each other. Some were brutal men, but the best knights used their privileged position to set high standards of courage and honor.

In legends about King Arthur, the brave young knight Percival (above) helped in the search for the Holy Grail.

King Arthur sits with his Knights of the Round Table. Lancelot is on the king's right and Percival on his left. The Round Table stood in the great hall of a legendary castle. Since the table had no head, all the knights seated around it were of equal rank. They were all bound by oath to help each other in times of danger and never to fight among themselves.

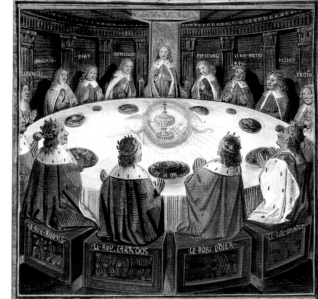

Arthurian legend
Legendary tales about King Arthur and his knights came originally from Celtic sources and were very popular during the Middle Ages. In the 12th century a Welsh priest, Geoffrey of Monmouth, wrote down some of the stories and a French poet, Chrétien de Troyes, wrote poems about similar legends. A German romance of 1212 by Wolfram von Eschenbach tells the tale of Percival's search for the Holy Grail, the cup supposedly used by Christ at the Last Supper. Arthurian tales are full of the knights' brave, heroic deeds and adventures.

A squire was dubbed a knight by his lord, or sometimes even by his king. At the investiture ceremony, the knight knelt before his lord and received a tap on the shoulder with his sword. This solemn occasion was often followed by a great feast of celebration.

This type of flat-topped helmet was worn by crusaders and other knights from the early 13th century. It covered the head completely, leaving two narrow eye slits. The reinforcing strips across the front form the shape of a crusader cross. Since this large helm was not a tight fit, there was no need for breathing holes.

This head of a crusader knight from around 1300 shows clearly how he protected his neck and ears with chain mail. The helmet was placed on top of the hood of mail. By this time many knights wore whole suits of mail beneath their plate armor.

This 14th-century miniature shows a new knight having his sword and spurs put on after his investiture. This was done to show that the knight was ready to fight on behalf of his lord. The ceremony meant a great deal to a young knight, who had probably spent about seven years as a page in a nobleman's household, and then another seven years serving another knight as a squire. At last he had a chance to put all his training into practice.

Mounted knights wore spurs on their heels to urge their horses on and encourage them to go faster. By the 15th century, spurs had spiked rotating wheels, called rowels. A knight's spurs had symbolic significance, and some were highly decorated.

The chain-mail shirt was often put on over a quilted vest, which gave extra protection. A plated armor breastplate might also be put on over the chain mail, making three layers of protection.

A piece of chain mail was made of thousands of small, linked iron rings. Armorers used pliers to join the links, adding or taking them away in separate rows to make the shape of chain-mail garments.

This 15th-century knight is wearing a full suit of armor. The metal armor was not as heavy as it looks. Armorers designed the plates so that they were jointed and allowed the wearer as much movement as possible. Even the foot armor, called sabatons, had a number of articulated plates so that the foot could move.

A knight's warhorse was an expensive, prized animal. The horse's head and flanks were often protected by chain mail and plate armor.

1. chanfron
2. crinet
3. peytral
4. flancard

This pointed helmet, called a basinet, had a hinged visor that covered the face and could be raised when there was no danger.

Simple prick spurs were made of a pointed piece of iron. A knight's spurs were put on top of mail or armor and attached to the ankle with leather straps.

Crossbows were very powerful but difficult to load. For small crossbows (left) a special lever was used to pull back the bowstring, but for larger versions a winding machine was used. Crossbowmen shot strong, short bolts.

This Norman infantryman at the Battle of Hastings, in 1066, was armed with a sword and a spear and was protected by a chain-mail suit, helmet, and shield. The Norman army also had cavalrymen and archers. King Harold of England was killed by a Norman arrow.

Siege warfare
Sieges formed an important part of medieval warfare because castles were built to be easily defended. Sometimes attacking armies would simply surround the castle, cut off supplies, and wait for the starving defenders to give in and come out – after days, weeks, or even months. Alternatively, attackers would try to force their way in, using battering rams, huge wooden catapults, and ladders.

In this miniature, the attackers are protected by a wheeled cover as they chip away at the walls of the besieged castle. They might tunnel their way in or force the wall to collapse. Defenders throw down rocks and boiling oil.

The trebuchet was a large wooden catapult worked by weights. It had a winding mechanism to pull the long arm down. A big stone was then put in the sling at the end of the arm. Weights at the other end made the long arm swing over and hurl the stone through the air.

Knight's ransom
Knights often made war pay by capturing enemies rather than killing them. A captured enemy could be held for ransom, an amount of money or goods that depended on the wealth and importance of the captive. When King John II of France was taken prisoner by a group led by Edward the Black Prince at Poitiers in 1356, he told his English captors that he was so great a lord that his ransom would make them all rich. Sadly, however, it turned out that he was unable to raise the amount they demanded.

Longbows were accurate and deadly weapons in the hands of experts. A longbowman could shoot many arrows in the time it took to reload a crossbow. He fired long, wooden arrows with feather flights.

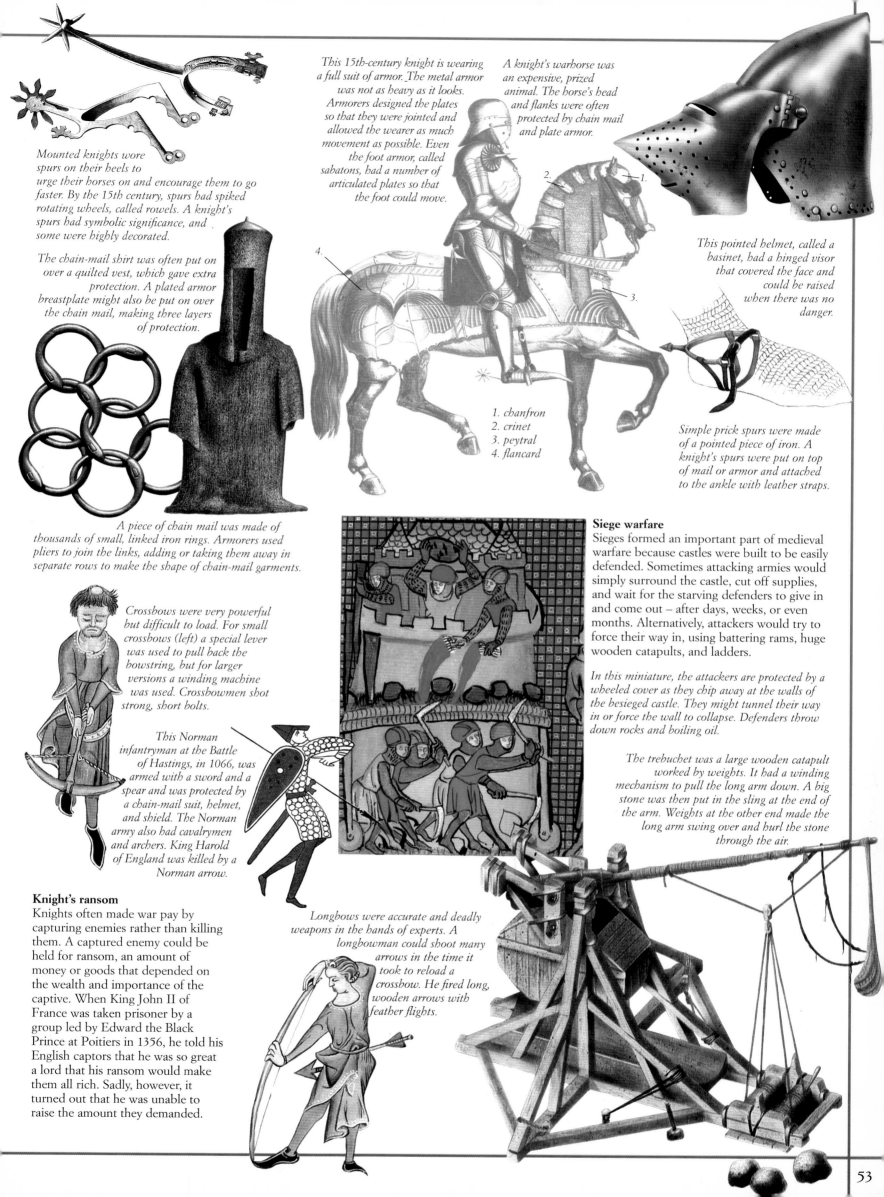

The medieval lute was like an early guitar. It was played by minstrels who sang songs about love and the brave deeds of knights.

Long-toed shoes were made of flexible goatskin, with a tough cowhide sole. The best soft leather came from Cordoba, in Spain.

Bagpipes were popular in Europe and in parts of Asia and Africa. The player blew into the short pipe to fill the windbag with air. Then he pressed the bag under his arm to push air into the sounding pipes.

Music and Entertainment

Music, song, and dance were popular forms of entertainment with all classes during the Middle Ages. Few people could play a musical instrument, and those that could traveled round courts, fairs and grand houses to entertain people. Many different kinds of musical instruments were played, many of which are similar to those still used today. Troubadours wrote and sang about love and chivalry, while minstrels entertained guests at banquets and festivals. Hunting with hounds and falcons was a favorite pastime for the rich, and they used their prey to please their cooks and fill their kitchens. Ordinary people generally had far too much work to do to think much about having fun, but villagers did sometimes play ball games. In medieval times these were disorganized, violent events.

This page (below) from an English book of music dates from about 1420. It shows how developed musical notation was in the Middle Ages.

At high table

French troubadours and German minnesingers were poet-musicians who wrote and sang songs, especially about love. They and other minstrels entertained lords and ladies at banquets and other events. This minstrel (below) is playing a medieval fiddle called a "rebec." The diners are sitting at the "high" table, which was raised on a platform so that the most important guests could look down on those at the ordinary, lower tables. At a banquet, servants would bring several courses of meat dishes, fish, and poultry, followed by sweet puddings.

Jesters entertained their audience by telling jokes, pulling faces, and generally clowning around. A favorite jester was often kept at a royal court to act as a "fool," making people laugh and helping them to forget the problems of everyday life.

Medieval Europeans celebrated weddings, holidays, and other special occasions with folk dances. Both adults and children performed sword dances and danced around maypoles. The nobility developed more elegant versions of the peasants' folk dances, as shown here in a painting by the Italian artist Ambrogio Lorenzetti (c.1290–1348). Lords and ladies often performed a circle dance called a carol.

Young men played a simple kind of hockey during the Middle Ages. This 14th-century version (below) used bent sticks and a large leather ball.

In noble houses, people wanted privacy for themselves and their valuable belongings. The 15th-century lock (right) shows the level of decoration that was put into ordinary metal objects. It bears the inscription IHS. The keys from the same period are beautifully made.

This leather purse has a highly decorated iron frame and clasp. Such fashion accessories replaced ordinary cloth pouches for carrying coins and provided a new market for craftsmen and traders.

Sports and pastimes

Ball games were popular in the Middle Ages, including bowls, hockey, and soccer. In England, whole villages challenged each other to rowdy games of soccer. By the 1300s the game was banned twice by English kings – first for being too rough, and then for stopping young men from practicing their archery. One nobleman described soccer as "more common, undignified and worthless than any other kind of game!" Archery and wrestling were also very popular, and an early form of cricket was probably played in England during the 1300s.

This medieval chessboard is made of ivory and inlaid wood. The knight is also ivory.

Tournaments originated in France in the 11th century. At these exciting festivals, knights competed in various tests of skill and courage, including jousting with lances.

In the 15th century wealthy ladies wore long gowns, often trimmed with ermine, marten, or sable fur, and they were fond of the beautiful silks brought from China. Favorite headgear was the tall, cone-shaped hennin, with a veil attached.

Falconry, or hawking, was a popular sport during the Middle Ages. Falcons, hawks, and kestrels were trained to catch rabbits or doves, and then return to their owner. Falconers wore a thick leather glove so that the birds could perch on their fist.

Chess

Chess was brought to Spain by Muslims in the 8th century and had spread across Europe by 1000. The pieces are taken straight out of medieval life: the king, queen, castles, knights, bishops, and pawns (foot soldiers).

A lord and lady stand under the spell of courtly love. This was a favorite theme for songs and poems, and it was governed by special rules of chivalry. A noble knight usually worshiped his lady from afar.

Tristan and Isolde

A medieval German poet, Gottfried von Strassburg (c.1170–1220), wrote a famous poem called Tristan and Isolde. In the poem, Tristan and Isolde drink a magic love potion by mistake and fall in love. However, Isolde is married to a king, and her love for Tristan ends in tragedy. Over 600 years later, the German composer Richard Wagner (1813–83) (left) used the medieval poem as the basis for his famous opera, also called Tristan and Isolde.

Hunting

Hunting was considered a noble pursuit. Lords and ladies enjoyed riding on horseback, chasing deer, wild boar, and other animals through their own woodland. They kept packs of hounds specially for this purpose. Peasants were not allowed to take part. There were special hunting rules, which young squires had to learn. For example, a male deer was usually only hunted when he was over five years old.

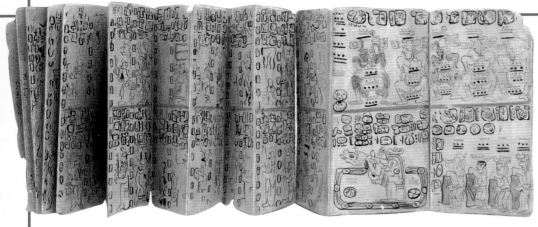

The Mayas wrote using hieroglyphs like the ones shown here (left). Archaeologists have only recently learned how to read Mayan writings.

The Rest of the World

Throughout most of this book we have focused on events and people in Europe and the Near East. But important and exciting things were happening elsewhere in the long arc of time between 500 and 1500. In the Far East, the vast Chinese Empire was reunited again in the 6th century and, under three major dynasties, stayed that way until the Mongols burst on to the scene in 1279. Their period of domination was relatively brief, and the powerful Ming dynasty restored unity in 1368. The Americas, unknown to Europeans throughout most of this time (except to a handful of Viking explorers), were inhabited by a huge number of independent nations, some of whom, like the Incas and the Mayas, had built extraordinarily complex and developed civilizations.

Far out in the Pacific Ocean, over 2,000 miles east of Chile, lies tiny Easter Island. The island was first inhabited from about AD 400. Over the following thousand years the inhabitants carved and erected tall statues. Although there are many theories and legends about these mysterious figures, no one knows why they were built.

Settlers arrived in ancient North America from Asia during the last Ice Age. By the time of the European Middle Ages they had spread out over the whole northern continent. Many groups lived nomadic lives and survived by hunting, gathering, and fishing; other groups were settled farmers.

NORTH AMERICA

The Toltec civilization flourished in central Mexico from about AD 900 to 1200. The Toltecs built tall, pyramid-shaped temples from which to worship their gods.

The Mayas lived in modern southern Mexico, Guatemala, and Belize. Their civilization dates to long before the birth of Christ, but reached its peak in the time between AD 200 and 900.

SOUTH AMERICA

Terracotta statue of a royal couple, carved at Ife (in modern Nigeria) during the 12th century.

The Aztec civilization of central Mexico emerged in about 1428. It was destroyed just under one hundred years later by Cortés and the Spaniards. This statue shows an Aztec god.

When Spanish explorer Francisco Pizarro arrived in the Andes, the Incas ruled over a huge empire that stretched from modern Colombia to central Chile.

Warrior king Mansu Musa from Mali greets a Muslim merchant.

The Pre-Columbian civilizations

The term "Pre-Columbian civilizations" refers to the Native American groups in Mexico, Central America, and the Andean region before the arrival of Spanish explorers in the 16th century. These civilizations rivaled the ancient Egyptians, Chinese, and Mesopotamians for their brilliance and level of development. The Mayas, Aztecs, and Incas are among the best known of these groups. All three civilizations reached their zenith during the thousand years of European history that we called the Middle Ages. Tragically, they were all destroyed by the arrival of European conquerers.

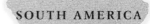

The birth of printing

The first book was printed in China during the 9th century, using a woodblock technique. About 150 years later the Chinese inventor Bi Sheng invented the first movable-type printing system.

Chinese civilization flourished under the Tang dynasty (AD 618–907). The Tang capital of Chang'an, with over one million inhabitants, was the largest city in the world in 750. This colorful horse dates from the Tang dynasty.

1.

2.

4.

3.

*1. Ink and water are mixed together in a shallow dish.
2. Ink is applied to columns of characters.
3. A sheet of paper is placed over the inked characters and rubbed with a pad. 4. The paper is peeled away, revealing the ink characters printed on it.*

A period of disunity followed the collapse of Tang rule, but by 960 the Song dynasty (960–1279) had restored order. Science, art, and many kinds of learning progressed in China throughout medieval times. In many ways Chinese civilization was in advance of its European counterpart. This vase (left) was made during the Song dynasty.

The spread of Buddhism

Although the founder of Buddhism lived about five centuries before Christ, for a long time there were few Buddhists outside of India. During the Middle Ages Buddhism gained wide popularity in China, Japan, Tibet, and Southeast Asia. A flexible religion, Buddhism adapted to local beliefs and took on different forms and names. The Islamic and Hindu faiths also spread through much of Asia at this time.

Medieval India saw the rise and fall of many regional kingdoms. There was a strong revival of the Hindu religion, while Buddhism declined. Islam spread, and repeated Islamic attempts to conquer India were successful in the north from about 1200.

ASIA

E

Despite attempts to unite the country under the emperor, power in Japan remained divided among several warrior clans. Wars often occured and the culture of the warrior, or samurai appeared. Samurai wore elaborate suits of armor.

Polynesian settlers traveled thousands of miles in the vast Pacific Ocean in strong canoes.

Many stable kingdoms and large empires had emerged in Southeast Asia by about 1000. The Khmer Empire of Cambodia, which built a huge temple complex at Angkor, was one of the most powerful. Farther north, in modern Burma, the Burmese built another civilization around Pagan.

The mosque at Djénné, in Mali, built near the ancient market town of Jenne-jeno.

AUSTRALIA

The hunter and gatherer peoples of Australia continued to live as they had for thousands of years.

In New Zealand, the farthest corner from European influence, the Maori people came from Polynesia in ocean-going canoes. Settling the land in about 1200, they lived by a mixture of farming and hunting. The large flightless Moa was wiped out soon after their arrival.

The African kingdoms

The period between 500 and 1500 saw the rise of many chiefdoms, cities, and empires in sub-Saharan Africa. The earliest known kingdom appeared in Ghana in about 700. A lot more is known about the empire of Mali which arose about 600 years later. It was strongly influenced by the Muslim states north of the Sahara. Cities such as Timbuktu and Jenne-jeno, at the southern ends of the caravan routes across the Sahara, became important market towns. Farther south, the imposing kingdom of Great Zimbabwe arose in the 13th century.

Swahili traders plied the coast of east Africa in merchant boats called mtepe. They carried goods between East African markets and the Near East.

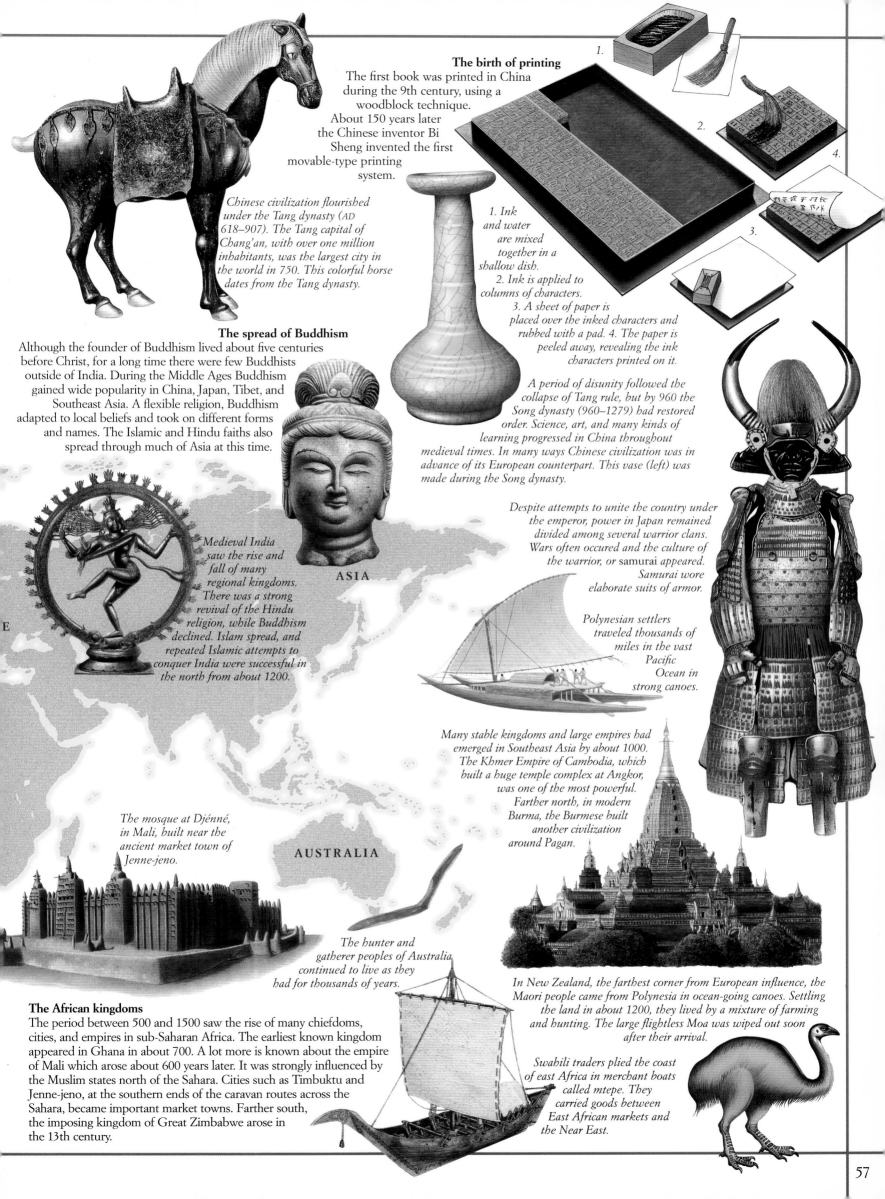

Europe Sets Sail

The European Middle Ages drew to a close in the 15th century as explorers sought new maritime trading routes to the East. In just a few short decades they found sea passages to India and Southeast Asia via Africa and the Red Sea. Almost by accident, they also "discovered" the Americas, which stood in their path as they set out due west from Europe in the direction, as they correctly believed, of the Far East. The initial disappointment of finding a huge land mass between themselves and their goal quickly turned to glee as they took measure of the immense wealth the Americas offered. This led to new voyages of exploration and conquest that increased in number and scope with the dawn of the 16th century. Contact and trade between Europe and the rest of the world increased immensely and Europe's role in world affairs grew accordingly.

Christopher Columbus, an experienced sailor and navigator, believed that the world was round and that if he sailed westward across the Atlantic he would reach the fabled lands of Japan and China. Many people thought he was crazy but some, including the king and queen of Spain, who financed his expedition in 1492, believed him. Columbus landed in the present-day West Indies, although he believed that he had reached the coast of China. Columbus made three more journeys to America; he died firmly convinced that he had discovered the western sea route to the Far East.

Improvements in maritime technology were of fundamental importance to the European voyages of discovery in the 15th and 16th centuries. A new ship – the caraval – was invented. Long, narrow, and shallow, with square and triangular sails, it was light and easy to control. It could sail both inshore and close to the wind, making it perfect for long ocean voyages followed by the exploration of rugged coastlines and river mouths.

Trade and exploration

Trade was the main spur to exploration. Merchants particularly wished to reach the East where spices and other valuable goods were produced. The decline of the Mongol Empire made overland trade between Europe and Asia more difficult and the Europeans turned to the sea. The Portuguese and Spanish on the Atlantic coast were perfectly placed for voyages of discovery. Sailing down the west coast of Africa, they eventually rounded the Cape of Good Hope, crossed the Indian Ocean, and achieved their goal.

Vasco da Gama (c. 1460–1524), Portuguese explorer who opened up the sea route between Europe and the East. His three voyages (1497–99, 1502–03, 1524, took him down the west coast of Africa, around the Cape of Good Hope and on to India. Vasco da Gama helped to make Portugal a world power in the 16th century.

The conquest of the Americas

Columbus's triumphant return to Europe led to many more voyages to America, mainly by Spaniards and Portuguese. Initially attracted by timber and sugar, they soon heard rumors of fabulously rich civilizations farther inland. In what became known as the "search for El Dorado" (the land of gold), *conquistadores* such as Cortés and Pizarro quickly conquered the Aztecs and Incas, whose arrows and spears were useless in the face of the Europeans' guns. The indigenous populations were soon subdued, although more died from the diseases which the Europeans carried than from gunshot.

Johannes Gutenberg (c.1398–1468), German craftsman who set up the first printing press using movable type in 1450.

Page from the first commercially printed book – The Gutenberg Bible, 1455.

Wealthy merchants and bankers sponsored works of art and building projects on a scale unknown since Classical times. When the Florentine artist Filippo Brunelleschi built the dome of Florence Cathedral in 1420–36 it was the first dome of its type to have been built in Europe since the fall of the Roman Empire.

Renaissance princes, such as Lorenzo the Magnificent of Florence, established Renaissance courts where scholars and artists met to discuss the new learning and ideas.

The printing revolution

Gutenberg's invention spread quickly throughout Europe. In 1475 William Caxton introduced the technique into England. The invention of the printing press had far reaching consequences. Before, books were laboriously copied out by hand and were rare and expensive. Now, books and the ideas they contained, became relatively cheap and available to large numbers of people. When the German monk Martin Luther (1483–1546) published his criticisms of the Catholic Church many people read them and agreed with him. This eventually led to the Reformation.

Humanism and the Renaissance

Beginning in Italy in the 14th century, more and more scholars looked back at the Greek and Roman worlds as ideal times when knowledge, art, and learning were accorded their true worth. They collected Classical works, studied Greek and Latin authors and artists, and set out to imitate them. The result was an enormous expansion of learning and artistic creation centered initially on Italy, but which later spread throughout Europe. Much later, this time became known as the Renaissance, which means "rebirth," because it was believed that knowledge and art returned to the perfection of the Classical world after 1,000 years of darkness.

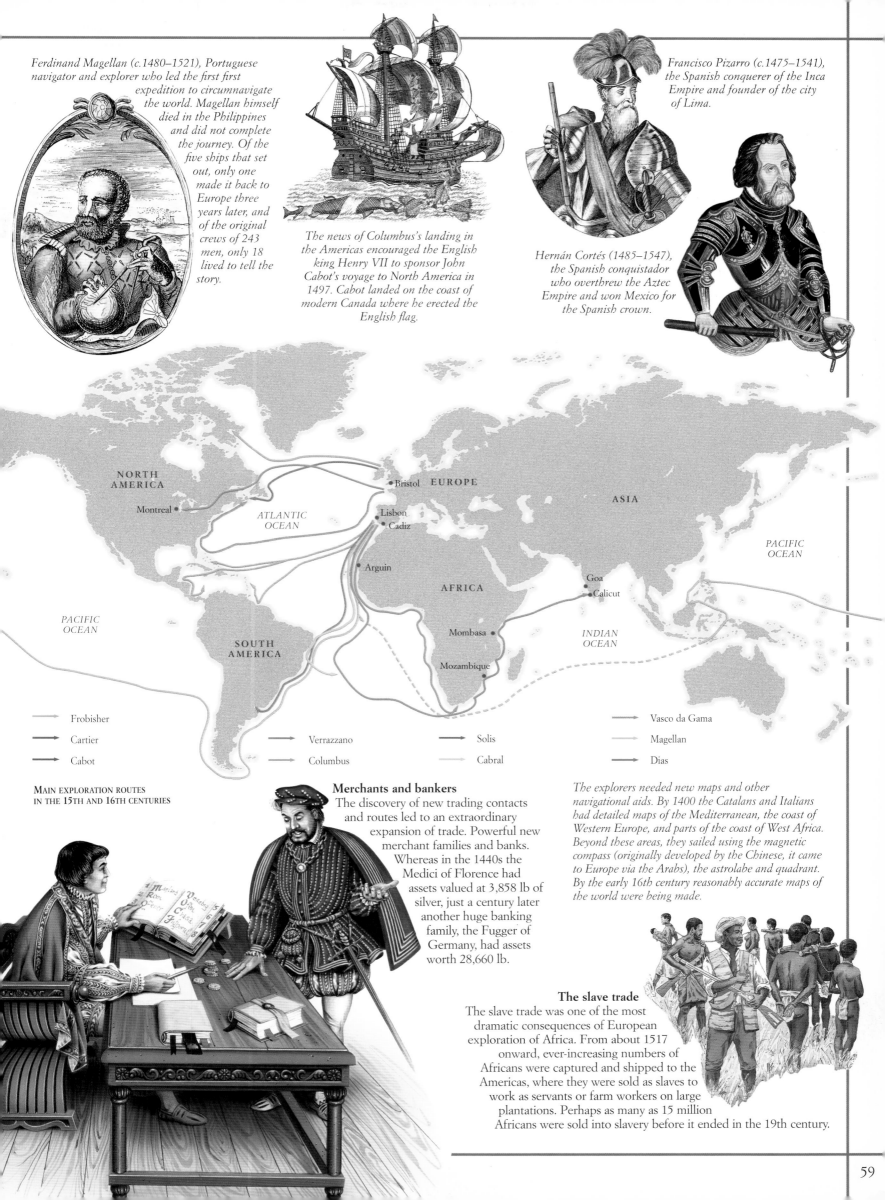

Ferdinand Magellan (c.1480–1521), Portuguese navigator and explorer who led the first first expedition to circumnavigate the world. Magellan himself died in the Philippines and did not complete the journey. Of the five ships that set out, only one made it back to Europe three years later, and of the original crews of 243 men, only 18 lived to tell the story.

The news of Columbus's landing in the Americas encouraged the English king Henry VII to sponsor John Cabot's voyage to North America in 1497. Cabot landed on the coast of modern Canada where he erected the English flag.

Francisco Pizarro (c.1475–1541), the Spanish conquerer of the Inca Empire and founder of the city of Lima.

Hernán Cortés (1485–1547), the Spanish conquistador who overthrew the Aztec Empire and won Mexico for the Spanish crown.

MAIN EXPLORATION ROUTES IN THE 15TH AND 16TH CENTURIES

Merchants and bankers

The discovery of new trading contacts and routes led to an extraordinary expansion of trade. Powerful new merchant families and banks. Whereas in the 1440s the Medici of Florence had assets valued at 3,858 lb of silver, just a century later another huge banking family, the Fugger of Germany, had assets worth 28,660 lb.

The explorers needed new maps and other navigational aids. By 1400 the Catalans and Italians had detailed maps of the Mediterranean, the coast of Western Europe, and parts of the coast of West Africa. Beyond these areas, they sailed using the magnetic compass (originally developed by the Chinese, it came to Europe via the Arabs), the astrolabe and quadrant. By the early 16th century reasonably accurate maps of the world were being made.

The slave trade

The slave trade was one of the most dramatic consequences of European exploration of Africa. From about 1517 onward, ever-increasing numbers of Africans were captured and shipped to the Americas, where they were sold as slaves to work as servants or farm workers on large plantations. Perhaps as many as 15 million Africans were sold into slavery before it ended in the 19th century.

Index